The Beauty of a Grieving Mother

Mothers Share their Stories of Finding Hope after the Loss of a Child

Curated by Elly Sheykhet

Alina's Light Publishing

Pittsburgh, PA

The Beauty of a Grieving Mother: Mothers Share their Stories of Finding Hope after the Loss of a Child

Published by
Alina's Light Publishing

ISBN: 978-1-62375-193-7

Printed in the United States of America

Cover design by Karen Captline, BetterBe Creative
Edited by Allison Hrip, Aurora Corialis Publishing

www.alinaslight.com

DISCLAIMER

The advice and strategies found within this book are for informational purposes only, are made without guarantee on the part of the authors or the publisher, and may not be suitable for every situation. This work is sold with the understanding that neither the authors nor the publisher or those who worked on this book can be held responsible for results from any advice given in this book. The authors and publisher disclaim any liability in connection with the use of this information. The information contained in this book is not intended as a substitute for consultation with doctors, therapists, financial advisors, or other licensed professionals or advisors. The reader should consult a licensed professional to discuss a plan for addressing their specific lives, particularly relating to symptoms that may require diagnosis or medical attention, as necessary. The views and opinions expressed in this work are those of the individual authors only and do not necessarily reflect the official policy, view or position of the publisher or any other agency, organization, employer or company. The use of this book implies your acceptance of this disclaimer.

DEDICATION

This book is dedicated to all the beautiful children in Heaven and their beautiful mothers on Earth who walk their life journeys with ugly shoes on their feet but bright smiles on their faces.

SHINING LIGHTS
EARTH
GRADUATES

ALINA
7.07.1997
10.08.2017

MIA
01.05.2020
02.07.2020

EMMA
07.25.2003
04.07.2019

AMORA
03.10.1999
10.07.2017

NICHOLAS
06.19.1998
11.14.2017

AMANDA
05.03.1996
04.24.2017

RYAN
04.26.1995
08.22.2016

COLIN
02.11.1996
04.21.2017

AUSTIN
01.01.1996
12.29.2017

AARON
11.15.1987
09.22.2019

TABLE OF CONTENTS

FOREWORD

By Elizabeth Boisson

President and Co-Founder, Helping Parents Heal

www.HelpingParentsHeal.org

Having a child pass is one of the most challenging experiences that any parent can endure. I have had two children transition: my daughter Chelsea soon after she was born in Montpellier, France, in 1991, and my son Morgan at the Base Camp of Mt. Everest in Tibet in 2009.

Elly Sheykhet and these nine other beautiful Shining Light moms have not only learned to survive, but to thrive, after the passing of their children. In our international support group, Helping Parents Heal, we do not consider ourselves to be "bereaved," which is easily one of the saddest words in the dictionary. We feel connected with our children on the other side. We know that their incredible lights shine through us, illuminating us and all those around us.

A dear friend and talented evidential medium, Suzanne Giesemann, coined the phrase "Shining Light Parent," and it quickly became a part of the vernacular of our group. As Suzanne so aptly says, our kids are "still right here." They share in everything we do, and they hold our hands as we walk down the path to healing. They are our biggest cheerleaders, and they are now happy, healthy, and whole. Moreover, we do not refer to our children as "lost" or "gone"; instead, we speak of them in the present tense. We feel that our kids are now "home" and we are still "in school." And we have so much to learn while we are here!

I am grateful that Elly has created this inspiring collection of stories with other members of Helping Parents Heal, and I know that it will positively impact many parents and families. Like Elly, many of these moms donate their time and energy to helping parents who are newer on the journey. We believe that parents who have had a child transition are all part of one big family; our kids are now best friends, and they connect us here on earth. I cannot wait to hug each one of them someday.

But for now, there is a lot to do. Elly, Angela, Michelle, Tracy, Ramona, Camille, Holly, Claudia, Tammy, and Shari, are leading the way with helpful, practical tools to navigate this new way of life, with one foot here on earth and one foot on the other side. Their easy-to-read stories demonstrate how to find the "collateral beauty" sent by our children in spirit; the beautiful signs and validations we learn to identify and cherish.

If you have had a child pass, please know that you are not alone. Every service offered through Helping Parents Heal is free of charge. From the Affiliate Group meetings and

Caring Listeners to the YouTube videos, monthly newsletters, and Facebook groups, we are here to help you move forward and heal. And as Elly and these nine moms have so eloquently illustrated through this beautiful work, our kids are with us every step of the way.

With love and appreciation,

Elizabeth Boisson

The Beauty of a Grieving Mother

INTRODUCTION

Losing a child is the biggest fear of any parent, but it is not a fear that we often think about. We may wonder how we would handle life if we suffered a loss like our job, a parent, a partner, a dog, and many other "normal" losses. These are the ones we often face and fear during our lives.

Losing a child is not one of those.

Our human brain with its logical thinking does not dare to wonder about such a cruel contradiction of life. I believe you get this fear ONLY when your child gets sick with a life-threatening disease OR when you witness a close family who has lost their child. Your mind then starts panicking, trying to comprehend how it is even possible. That's when it becomes your biggest fear, and you start praying that it will never happen to *you*.

When you start "wondering" what your life would look like, your body immediately gets overwhelmed with intensive imaginary pain that you think would be impossible to survive. That's exactly what happened to me one day.

I had never feared losing my children. That thought had never even crossed my mind. I knew I was a good mother, and my kids were raised in a loving environment. I always thought about how healthy and beautiful my kids are, so I believed that nothing could ever happen to them. I was that optimistic, confident, and trusting.

I remember when my nineteen-year-old daughter had delivered me the shocking news that a student at her alma matter was murdered. We had a long emotional conversation, both feeling sorry for that young man and his family. My daughter could not stop saying how unbelievable that event was. Suddenly, she became silent and looked away, pensive. Then she mischievously smiled at me, and joked, "Mom, what if it was ME?"

I did not expect to be asked such a horrifying question, and I felt as if I had just been shocked by a Taser. For one short second, I wondered what it would feel like and almost fainted as the fear paralyzed my whole body and mind. In that moment, I truly believed there would be no way I could survive my life without my child. That thought became my biggest fear that I franticly pushed away every time it haunted my mind. I was only comforted by my faith that God is good, so he will never let it happen to my kids.

But despite my optimism, trust, and prayers, it *did* happen to one of my children. One year later, my daughter's joke— "Mom, what if it was ME?"—had become my reality. It was HER—my daughter, my child, my baby—who was murdered this time. My world had collapsed, and my life became shrouded in the biggest fear of all mothers.

Please, do not get discouraged by what I'm sharing here. This book is NOT about fear.

In this anthology, ten broken-hearted mothers step ahead of their fears and share their life stories about love, courage, hope, and survival. All those moms are dear friends whom I connected with through the club no one wants to join: the club of bereaved parents. We all ten are different—different lifestyles and backgrounds—but we all walk the same journey and share a special bond of carrying our children in our hearts. Our stories are all different, our kids have left in different ways and at different ages, and we all grieve differently. But what makes us the same is the deepest feeling of love for our beautiful children and a strong desire to continue their legacies.

We, grieving mothers, try hard to move forward in life. But we want you to know that it does not mean we move AWAY from our children; we move forward WITH them. Although they are not here physically, we know that they still stand by us every day. And not only do we cherish our old memories, but we also create new ones.

I truly believe that such a heartfelt book project will become one of everlasting memories because we have written this book together with our children. They guided and inspired us in the writing process, and it brought us so much healing.

In my eyes, this book appears as a beautiful piece of healing art—the collaborative work of two amazing teams—forever loving moms on Earth and their incredible children in Spirit. I hope this book will also bring light and healing to the broken hearts of many others.

ALINA

The Power of Love

If you Google the meaning of the name "Alina," you'll find that it means:

> Independent and strong-willed. Alina is a free-spirited, ambitious girl. Even though she knows where she is going, it is not clear where she has been. Her origin is debatable, and the name means something different in different countries and cultures. In Armenia, it means "bearer of light." In Arabic it means "illustrious." In France, it is defined as "noble." Whatever its meaning, Alina has lots of positive energy and a bright future.[1]

My daughter Alina was born in Russia. I had never Googled her name, but its meaning resembles exactly who my daughter was for the 20 years of her life on Earth. She was a bright, beautiful light, and that light has never dimmed . . .

Alina was a very well-planned baby. Because my husband and I already had a son, we looked forward to having a daughter. One hot summer day, July 7, 1997, God answered our prayers by sending us a precious baby girl. It really seemed as if Alina had come into our family as a gift from God. As she grew, I often wondered what I had done to be given such a special gift. I always thought I was just one lucky mother.

Alina had always been special. She always stood out from the crowd. She started walking at 8 months, and when she was 2, she read poetry at the holiday concerts at her daycare. She was a gifted child and always thought and talked as if she were

---

[1] "Alina," The Bump, accessed March 26, 2021, https://www.thebump.com/b/alina-baby-name

older than her age. I was amazed by her ability to know everything. She always told us about the latest world's news and advised us in different areas of life. I often joked with her, asking who the real mother was, because she often acted as if she were a mother to me. She was my best friend and had taught me so much.

Amazingly, Alina could have a nice conversation with anyone, no matter their age, background, or even mood. She never tried to be something or someone she wasn't. She was always authentic in anything she was doing. She was REAL—a smart, intelligent, funny, open-minded, and big-hearted beautiful girl with a big bright smile on her face.

When our family moved to the United States, Alina was only 3 and a half. She was always the tiniest one in school. I remember one day she came home crying because she got bullied by her classmates. The tears running down her sad face seemed bigger than she was. "Mommy, why did you and Dad have to make me so small?! I look like an undeveloped child. Everybody laughs at me, saying how ugly I am and that no one would ever want to be friends with me." She looked adorable in my eyes.

I hugged her tightly and wiped a puddle of tears off her sweet little face. I remember having a long conversation with her that day. I explained that some kids put others down because it makes them feel better about themselves. I emphasized how smart and beautiful she is. I explained that being small is actually a good thing because most men prefer petite women and that she can wear the highest heels in the world when she grows up. That made her laugh, because she loved trying on my high-heeled shoes and could not wait to wear them one day.

On a serious note, I explained that what makes any girl beautiful is her big heart. "You're a very smart girl, and you are always kind to your friends. That is important. I love you so much and want you to know that your daddy and I are so proud of our little girl because you have the biggest heart in the world. And as long as your heart remains big, your real friends would never hurt you, no matter how small your body is." I told her to ignore those mean boys and keep smiling. And that is what she did for the rest of her life. She always smiled, even when she was hurting. It seemed she was afraid of nothing. She always knew what she wanted in life and never gave up.

Alina was a talented dancer. She started dancing when she was 4 and danced her whole life. Her dance activities kept us busy. She danced like no one could stop her. We always traveled as she participated in different concerts and events. Our family and friends enjoyed watching our little peanut perform. She was an amazing dancer, and she knew it. But also, she believed that she was a "horrible" singer. She loved singing, but the only place where she was able to open her mouth was the shower. Singing on stage one day was her biggest dream, but at the same time, this thought petrified her with fear because she thought she "had no voice." As luck would have it, an owner of Alina's dance school, a professional Broadway tap dancer, saw a great potential in Alina to be a "triple threat"—a strong dancer, actor, and singer. She made Alina believe that she was a beautiful singer and helped her overcome her fear of singing in public.

When Alina was in seventh grade, she auditioned for a dancer part in her school musical. The audition required singing as well. Oh boy, to say she was nervous during auditions is nothing. She was shaking like a leaf while waiting for her name to be called, and I was shaking with her thinking, "My poor girl, why would you need to get yourself involved in such a nerve-racking event?!" Despite her fear, she was determined to be a dancer in *Thoroughly Modern Millie*.

I remember how one day soon after tryouts she came home from school crying like a child. "OMG, mom you will not believe it!" She sounded as if she did not get a part in the show, so I held her tight, consoling her. I told her that she could try again next year. "No mom, you don't understand!" She seemed panicked as she handed me the cast list. "Look, Mom, it says 'Millie' next to my name. OMG, what am I going to do now? I got the lead role, and I cannot sing on stage." I started crying too, overwhelmed with love and pride for my sweet little Millie. I knew she deserved it.

Her performance was amazing. Alina looked the smallest on stage, but her beautiful voice filled the auditorium. The audience was in awe of how such a powerful voice could come from such a tiny body. Our shy little girl had turned into a beautiful actress. After that, she starred in several musicals and plays, bringing tears, smiles, and much applause while on stage.

When Alina was 14, she suffered a severe knee injury during a ballet class that prevented her from pursuing her passion as a dancer and performer. However, her injury treatment experience inspired her to become a doctor of physical therapy.

Alina spent the first two year of her college career at the University of Pittsburgh-Greensburg, where she met a guy who, in her words, "treated her like a princess," and that is why she liked him so much. My husband and I did not take that relationship seriously, assuming that it was just another date and she was not going to marry him. What we did not know—what Alina was hiding from us—is that she was controlled and mentally abused by that person. She tried to break up with him several times but was manipulated and had to continue that toxic relationship. Our family did not know how bad her relationship was. I believe she did not want to upset us and thought she would resolve all her issues on her own.

One night we received a phone call from her saying that she had to call the police because her ex-boyfriend broke into her house and demanded that she talks to him. Alina was transferred to the main campus in Pittsburgh at that time and lived in a rented off-campus house with her friends. That was when she shared how badly she had been treated and that she needed to file a protection from abuse order (PFA). I was in shock. I would have never thought that my sweet, loving, beautiful girl could be treated that way.

On October 5, 2017, my husband and I brought her to the courthouse to file the PFA. She thought she was protected by the law now, and we really thought that man would never bother her again. But the system failed our daughter. And we, as parents, failed our daughter by trusting the system and not taking the situation seriously enough.

Two days after, early on the morning of October 8, my husband and I found Alina in a pool of her own blood. The PFA did not stop that obsessive man from breaking into our daughter's house again and stilling her precious life. The enraged monster brutally destroyed Alina's body with a claw hammer so she could not be with anyone. That horrifying scene will haunt us for the rest of our lives. We had plans that day for a happy celebration for our older son's birthday. Instead, my family was devastated by such a tragic loss.

I honestly do not know how my husband and I survived that day. I felt as if I was an actress in a horror movie. Nothing felt real. I was numb from the moment I saw the unrecognizable body of my daughter. I felt as if I left my own body and was watching the scene from the side. I was in a deep state of shock.

My husband had a different reaction. The harsh reality hit him like a ton of bricks. He did not feel as if he were an actor, as I did; he experienced excruciating pain immediately. I watched him turning into a raging animal, hysterically punching the ground and threatening to kill himself and everyone there. I watched my son viciously fighting the policemen trying to get into the house to see his sister.

My brain was not able to comprehend what was happening around me. Everything moved in a slow motion. I felt as if an elephant were sitting on my chest. I could not breathe. My husband was sedated and taken to the psychiatric unit of the local hospital. As the ambulance was leaving the scene, I stared at my daughter's bedroom window, hoping it was just a bad dream and that she would wave at me. She did not wave. And the ambulance was taking us farther and farther from the house that was a second home for Alina and that had swallowed her and all her dreams forever.

What I felt in the next few days is hard to describe. Notifying our families and friends about what happened and making funeral arrangements was very painful. I truly believe that being in shock that whole time helped my heart survive. Had I not become numb, it would have shattered into a million pieces. My system was running on autopilot, and I had a hard time reconciling all those unrealistic events—choosing the best-looking casket for my daughter and the most beautiful dress she could wear for the last time ever. I felt as if it was a bad dream I desperately wanted to wake up from. As I looked at my daughter's breathless body lying in a casket and then watched it being closed and buried under the ground, I screamed inside, begging God to let me wake up. That bad dream lasted until after the funeral. The moment everybody left, and the dead silence filled in every tiny area of our house, I finally woke up to an everlasting nightmare. My daughter was really gone.

As days passed by, the shock wore off, and the reality sunk in deeper and deeper. Grief was overwhelming. I have felt every single emotion that normally comes with grief. You name it, I have had it. Those ugly feelings consumed my whole being, draining my body physically and emotionally so all I could do was blink. I did not have the energy to function at all.

I stayed in denial for so long. My brain understood that my daughter was gone, but my soul rejected such an unrealistic thought. I desperately did not want my daughter to be dead. Period. I felt very angry. No words could bring me comfort. I simply did not want my life to be turned in the direction it did. Having no control over my life made me insane. I felt frightened as never before. I felt as if I were dangled over the edge of a cliff and threatened to be dropped. I felt suffocated. I felt as if I were walking with no ground under my feet. I feared living.

I felt profoundly empty inside. I felt a huge hole in my chest, not only mentally but physically as well. I could almost feel the wind blowing through this hole. Nothing was inside me. I did not know who I was anymore. I lost my identity, my faith, my life purpose, and my future. By losing my daughter, I had lost my entire self. I did not feel like I belonged to this world anymore.

My husband and I thought about taking our own lives often . . . We both were in such a dark place and just wanted to escape it. I remember our talks about how to make it happen. We came up with many creative ideas for how to exit this life. We did not care about this world anymore or what would be left behind. As selfish as it sounds, it is a bitter truth. That is how the loss of a child makes you feel.

Both my husband and I felt extremely guilty for failing our daughter's life. "What ifs" and "should haves" drove us crazy. I constantly played past events in my mind, kicking myself for not having said this or not having done that. My poor husband put the blame fully on himself. He felt as if it was only his fault that his daughter was gone.

The other feeling eating us from the inside was hatred toward the person who deliberately murdered our child. Our whole family dreamed of revenge. We desperately wanted to make his family's life miserable for having raised a monster and giving him the green light to invade our daughter's privacy and destroy our family. Managing those forceful negative energies was very challenging. Despite our urge to make that family suffer, we never took any actions, of course. We knew nothing would bring our girl back. We realized that harm would have created even more harm, and healing could come from love only. That monster did not deserve to be the focus of our lives. Instead of hate for him and his family, we wanted to fill our hearts with love for Alina and to focus on keeping her memory alive.

At the one-year mark of the tragedy, Alina's murderer pleaded guilty and was sent to a prison where he will spend the rest of his life. We were blessed to have a case closed in a short period of time so we could concentrate on the nonprofit we had established in Alina's memory.

I knew my daughter's death was not in vain. I wanted her beautiful bright life to be honored in many ways. Although starting the organization in memory of our daughter was very painful, my husband and I knew that it was the only way to survive, because "moving on" was not an option for us. You cannot let go of your child; instead you must learn how to fit that horrifying event into your life as a "normal" daily thing and keep going. The biggest fear of a bereaved mother is that her child's name will be forgotten. I wanted Alina's name to be mentioned everywhere. We named our organization Alina's Light. It has become my child. Running Alina's Light feels as if I keep parenting my daughter, and it brings me sanity.

Honoring my daughter's life by helping others was not enough for me, though. It could not bring me peace. I desperately needed to know where my daughter had gone to. I had so many questions about life and was seeking answers. My research led me to the door of my daughter's new world—the beautiful world filled with Love, Hope, Spirit, and Gratitude. With no hesitation I opened it wide and started fluttering between two worlds—a physical world and a spirit world.

I learned that our grieving process depends on our belief systems. My old beliefs did not support my healing and survival. So, I have destroyed my old belief system and built a new one.

It is well known that acceptance is the last stage of grief. However, I found this term to be a misnomer because no parent would ever "accept" the death of their child.

When my grief counselor at the Center for Victims of Crime said to me, "I am not going to bring your daughter back," I knew immediately that I would never return to that place. I knew I would never heal my heart and soul without my daughter being by my side. So, I started searching for her.

I read a ton of books about the afterlife. I watched a million YouTube videos of people sharing their near-death experiences. I took several mediumship classes and became a very spiritual person. I developed a different understanding of life and death. I have found all the answers to my millions of questions that allowed me to bring my daughter "back to life" and keep my close relationship with her.

Instead of trying to accept her death, which is absolutely impossible, I have accepted the fact that she has taken a different form. I realized that she simply lost her body but her energy and her consciousness has survived. I have learned a new language, the beautiful language of spirits, and communicate with my daughter daily. We exchange our thoughts telepathically. Also, she sends me her beautiful signs. A bird staring at me through the window. A cloud shaped as a heart. A car passing by with Alina's lucky number 77 on its plate. A meaningful song on the radio. And many other signs that make me recognize her presence. My daughter and I are connected on a different level now, a much deeper level. I feel even closer to her than when she was here in her physical body. We do everything together. She continues being my light and inspiration and guides me in every step of my new life.

Sometimes I pleasantly feel that she controls my mind and body. I do things in life now that I have never been capable of. I sometimes feel her integrate her strong energy with mine so I begin acting in a way she would. She was not afraid of anything in life and was very confident. I was never that powerful. I have always had fears and insecurities and often asked her in awe, "Alina, where does all your power come from?" I have changed a lot since my daughter left this planet.

I am not the Elly that people knew when my daughter was here. That Elly perished under the ruins of my old world, and a new version of me was born. Now I live my life for both, myself and my daughter. I know that pieces of her heart lie in mine. I feel as if I adopted some of her best qualities. I became more loving and compassionate and less judgmental. I can look at life with the eyes of others and feel them with my soul. I have become more confident about myself and have overcome one of my biggest fears: public speaking.

I am not afraid of doing presentations and giving interviews anymore. Every time I stand up in front of the crowd, I feel my daughter's power. I feel fearless, just the way she was. It has become my mission to share Alina's story and help others. I want people to be aware that domestic violence is a real thing, and it does not discriminate. The spirit of my daughter always stands by my side and empowers me to deliver such an important message.

Also, my daughter helped me write my first book, *One Year After*. I really feel that Alina pushed me to write this book just to let everyone know that she has not really gone. She wanted me to deliver a message of hope to other grieving parents.

I never possessed exceptional writing skills, even in my own language. I always struggled with writing essays in school. So, when I got an urge to write a book, I thought it was weird. I knew I could not write. But that feeling was very strong; it drove me crazy. It felt like if I wanted to fly, but I knew I was not a bird and don't have wings. So, how can I? I truly believe that it was one of Alina's crazy ideas. I could hear her voice very clearly in my mind. "Do not worry, Mom. You'll be fine. Just do it."

One day, I was thinking about the title. I knew I would never write a book, but if I did, I wondered what its title would be. Almost instantaneously, I heard in my mind "One Year After." I had a clear picture imprinted in my mind of how I would write it. I saw that it would have two parts, and I knew exactly the outline of the chapters. I thought I was losing my mind. The urge to write was very strong, and I was not able to stop it.

One day, I sat at the computer and typed the title. Then, shockingly, the story started unfolding. I did not struggle with the English as much as I thought I would. I felt as if some channel had opened, and all the thoughts started flowing.

I felt very emotional. I had to relive all those traumatic events again. As my fingers typed, I felt that excruciating pain again. I cried so many tears that I was not able to release at the time of those events. With each chapter finished, I magically felt peace. The warm, positive energy pleasantly flowed through my body, making me feel Alina's presence very strongly. I felt so much love and gratitude and could not explain why. I found writing very therapeutic. It helped me release the stuck negative energies from my body.

I know I am going to grieve until the moment I exit this world, but I learned how to shift a "normal" ugly grief to a different way of grieving. A "healthy" way. I learned how to transform the power of pain into the power of love. I truly believe that when we suffer, we activate our God-given power. But it is up to us how we use it.

I want to share my way of dealing with a grief wave. We, grieving parents, all know that grief comes in waves. When it hits you hard and you feel like drowning, try to do the following. Do not fight it. Acknowledge it. Just let it be. Feel all the pain and emotions. Tell yourself, "Grief is love with no place to go. I grieve because I love." Remind yourself that you suffer because you cannot express love to your child. And when you feel like you have had enough of that pain, focus on the best memories of your child. Sit with those memories for a while. Feel love.

Then make a positive shift. Instead of feeling separation and screaming, "My child is gone. I will never see my child again. I am forever broken," repeat a few times, "My child is still here but in a different form." Then try to feel oneness with your child. Feel his or her presence. Work with your mind and express that deep love through some action then. Do whatever you like doing: cooking, painting, writing, photography, whatever that is. Create something beautiful. Feel that you are doing it for your child, and that you are doing it together. Then, feel how much your child loves you back and how much they are proud of you. Finally, express gratitude for being able to connect with your child. That is what I personally do, and it helps tremendously.

But if you are brand new in this journey, please do not rush the process. All you can do is be gentle with yourself. This is like being in ICU with physical damage to your body. You need time to heal. You have a great mental trauma that needs to be healed before you can start doing "physical therapy."

Everyone goes through the grieving process differently. Just listen to yourself and do what feels right for you. I know you are madly saying now, "What are you talking about Elly? Nothing feels right?" And it is normal to feel that way. I have been there. Just do what your body needs. Cry, scream, swear, hit the wall with your fist, laugh. All those actions are normal. But also try to do something that stirs up positive emotions so your heart and soul can start healing.

And only when your mind and body feel stronger, make a commitment and confidently say, "Yes I want to heal; I am ready to heal." That's when you start working. For the rest of your life, your mind will have a hard daily job. You are a lifetime warrior now. But that is the only way to heal and move forward in life.

Losing a child is the most painful and devastating human experience. I believe it is one of the greatest challenges your soul can go through while being in a human body. But you are on earth to learn lessons and evolve. And the harder your challenge is, the more your soul grows.

I learned from many great teachers and healers that we are here in this physical realm for a reason. Our human body is literally just a programmed character that consciousness is utilizing to experience physical reality. No soul leaves a moment too soon or late. Our life span is exactly what our soul came here to experience. When it is time for our soul to leave, nothing or nobody can stop it or change it. All my studies, new beliefs, and personal experiences helped me make a huge shift in my grieving process. Instead of feeling like a victim of my life, I took all those circumstances as a great opportunity for my soul to grow and evolve.

Although I have had a few great experiences with mediums validating Alina's presence, I no longer need a medium now to tell me that my daughter's energy is all around me. I had a mind-blowing experience of past life regression where I recalled my past life and found out why I had to face such a great challenge in my current life. I share those amazing experiences in my book *One Year After*.

I am now a certified grief coach. It has become my mission and passion to guide and empower grieving parents as they navigate this difficult, yet rewarding journey to find hope, achieve growth, and maintain gratitude throughout their lives. All monies earned through my grief coaching service are donated directly to Alina's Light.

Also, I am blessed to be a volunteer Caring Listener at Helping Parents Heal, an organization that provides support to grieving parents all over the world. As a brand-new mom joining the club, I found HPH a vital piece for my survival. The amount of love, compassion, and understanding they give could not be found anywhere else. You can join an online group with thousands of parents in it or find one of their local groups for in-person meetings. I have met so many new friends there and gained so much knowledge about life and death through the stories of other members and a wonderful service provided by the organization that helped my healing process tremendously. As I walk my journey a few steps ahead of so many moms now, I want to lend a hand to those at the bottom of the grief hole trying to climb up to the surface.

Unfortunately, there is no manual for how to deal with the loss of a child. Grieving is a very scary, ugly, and confusing process. And from the beginning, you might feel that no one could ever help you. With all your being, you truly feel that nothing could ever stop that pain. You end up in a very dark place.

But I am living proof that survival is possible. Dear moms and dads, even if you feel hopeless right now, please believe that there *is* hope. I did not believe it myself, and I did not think I could survive. But I did.

My daughter taught me to light a candle instead of cursing the darkness. I can smile and feel joy again.

What I have learned from this journey is that pain can be the most powerful teacher. When we dive deep into the darkness of pain, we learn the greatest lessons in life. When the pain hurts immensely, it enables us to "see in the dark." The pain is now a part of who I am. But I respond to it with love. Love is the key. It is our greatest power that connects us with our loved ones on the other side. And I know for sure that even though they have passed on, they did not pass away. And my beautiful daughter is living proof to that.

I'll Never Accept that You're Gone

You're my breath in and my breath out
You make my heartbeat very loud
I'll never accept the fact you're gone
I'll never forget your smile and move on

Acceptance is one of the stages of grief
I don't believe it, that's such a myth
I won't accept such unnatural loss
It's unrealistic to accept the chaos

What I will accept—my pain never ends
My joy and my sorrow have become friends
Accept that I'll always miss you
Always craving to hug and kiss you

Accept the fact you're far away
Never standing in our doorway
Accept the fact you're in a different form
Accept the fact that you have transformed

I'll never accept that you are gone
I don't believe it, that's so wrong
I know your presence is still here
I feel your energy so near

I see your smile and hear your laugh
You're the same—beautiful, silly, tough
I know where to find you

The Beauty of a Grieving Mother

I know how to mind you

You taught me a new language you speak
I'm not afraid, my energy is not weak
Your energy is now very high
And you taught me how to fly

I learned how to quietly sit in a sacred patio
I learned how to tune in to your new radio
I switch my life radio to a different station
And here I am happy at your new location

I'll never accept the fact you're gone
That's such a lie, this statement is wrong
Death is not your ending
Death is your ascending

Your life continues at a higher level
You have no limits, there is no devil
You're happy and you're flying free
But still loving and always being with me . . .

Elly Sheykhet, Alina's Mom

Elly Sheykhet was born in Ivanovo, Russia, and spent her childhood alongside her parents and two brothers. After finding love and getting married, Elly moved to the United States in 2000 with her husband Yan and two beautiful children, Artem and Alina. Elly officially evaluated her Russian master's degree in economics in 2003 and then obtained her associate degree in accounting at Pittsburgh ICM School of Business. She is currently employed at Henderson Brothers, an insurance agency in downtown Pittsburgh and serves as their accountant and cash manager.

After losing her 20-year-old daughter Alina in a senseless act of violence in 2017, Elly and her husband founded Alina's Light, a nonprofit organization established in her memory. This organization is very dear to the Sheykhets and is often referred to by Elly as "her child."

The Beauty of a Grieving Mother

The mission of Alina's Light is to give voice to the victims of domestic violence through the arts, community events, and charitable actions. Elly is a published author and serves as a certified grief coach; she has dedicated her life to honoring her daughter by helping others. She hopes to brighten the world in Alina's memory.

Elly cherishes the time she spends with family and is a proud grandmother to Artem's daughter, Angelina.

Email: elly.sheykhet@alinaslight.com

Donations to Alina's Light are greatly appreciated.

https://alinaslight.com/

NICHOLAS

Chosen to Serve

If you're reading this book, chances are you have lost a child or know someone who has. If this is the case, I want to express my deepest, most heartfelt condolences. My hope is, while reading this, something may resonate with you as you try to sort through the overwhelming thoughts and emotions running through your entire being. Losing a child is a tragedy no mother should ever have to endure, and yet, here we are. I would like to dedicate this book to my one and only son, Nicholas Kole Novak. He will be forever 19 years old. One who has not only inspired his peers, but also me, to press forward to the finish line. One day soon, I'll meet him in glory. This is our story.

Our story starts as a fairytale of sorts: star-crossed lovers turned into happy husband and wife. You see, early in our marriage, Rick and I built our own company from the ground up. From the outside looking in, it appeared we had it all: a booming window tinting company, our dream home in the works, and a beautiful 9-year-old daughter. However, my husband and I always knew something was missing. We had tried to conceive another baby for years but had been unsuccessful, and we just assumed our daughter, Ashlee, would be our only child. However, when we were on vacation in Jamaica, I had this strange feeling that I had gotten pregnant.

I can't explain it; it was just a super-strange feeling. I told my husband that I had conceived, and he laughed because he thought I was joking. For the remainder of our trip, my conception remark was the new *inside joke*. So, you can imagine the shock when I saw my positive pregnancy test after we arrived back home. In the weeks following our vacation, my pregnancy was confirmed, and Rick and I were elated. I had an instant connection with this new life growing inside me. The connection between mother and child is like none other.

Nicholas was special from the very beginning, and conception was just the first of many miracles to follow. During my pregnancy I had six ultrasounds, all of which confirmed we had a healthy baby girl on the way. To hear that you have a healthy baby on the way is all one could ask for and I was so excited. Rick was grateful, but always had a gnawing feeling that our baby girl was in fact a baby boy. He was there for every ultrasound, and with a huge smile he would always point to my stomach and say, "Nope, it's not a girl. IT'S A BOY!" I thought it was a running joke among the two of us, but Rick was serious.

My husband was brought up in the Baptist church and was true in his faith. The Bible states, in Mathew 21:22, *And whatever things you ask in prayer, believing, you will receive.* (NKJV) Rick stuck to that verse and never wavered.

The morning of June 19, 1998, was like any other day at our business. The hustle and bustle of window tinting was ever present on this hot summer Friday, and while tinting a car door window, my water broke. I was terrified. My due date wasn't for another five weeks, on August 5th. Even though I had already been through one pregnancy and labor, I felt so scared this time. The baby was coming five weeks early and was still in the breech position. With the trifecta of chaos happening, and in my current state of confusion, I just hopped in the driver's seat of my car and headed to the hospital. The only thing running through my mind at the time was that my baby couldn't breathe, and I needed to get to the hospital as soon as possible.

I got about two miles down the road when my phone rang, and Rick asked, "Where are you?" I told him my water had broken and I was on my way to the hospital. He exclaimed, "GET BACK HERE SO I CAN DRIVE YOU! Are you crazy?" I hadn't gotten far, so I turned around and drove back to our shop where he was waiting outside. We made it to the hospital where the nurses confirmed that my water had indeed broken, and they began prepping me for a C-section.

I had been through this process before since our daughter Ashlee was also born via C-section. However, with her, I was not scared at all, even though I was ten years younger. Unlike Ashlee's birth, this baby was going to be premature: that terrified me. Before my mind could accept that I was about to have a preemie, the doctor entered the room, and it was time for our baby to make a grand appearance. As Rick made his way toward the operating room, the doctor asked if he was ready to meet his baby girl. To which he proudly responded, "Nope, I'm telling you, THAT is a boy right there. You watch and see."

I was all prepped for the arrival of my baby, with my husband by my side. The whole process felt like an eternity and a millisecond all at once. Our world was finally complete when the doctor proudly held my baby up and proclaimed, "Oh my goodness Rick, we're gonna have to circumcise something." With wide eyes and the largest smile I had ever seen, my proud husband shouted, "I TOLD YOU! I told you it was a boy. I knew it! My faith never wavered." Nicholas Kole Novak was born five weeks early, weighing in at 4lb. 8oz., and was whisked away to spend the next two weeks in the neonatal intensive care unit.

Those were the hardest two weeks of my life so far, having to leave my bundle of preciousness there, while I went home only to eat and shower. I was already so in love with everything about him. I was only 20 years old when I had his sister, and I felt like this was my second chance to do things differently with Nicholas. I held this child for what seemed like every minute of every day. I studied his tiny little features in detail, memorizing the way his perfect fingers intertwined together, and his beautiful full head of dark hair, piercing blue eyes, and those lips. I used to tell his grandma, "Those lips right there are gonna make some girl really happy." I was absolutely astonished that Rick and I could have ever made something so breathtakingly perfect. I stared at him for hours on end pondering the changes I would make from the regrets of my first child. I promised myself I would be a better mom to this little angel.

The newborn stage went by in a flash, and then we got to experience the wonder of our baby growing into a toddler, a preteen, and then a young man. We got to see his personality develop, and oh, what a wonder it was. As Nicholas began to grow into his little self, it became evident at an early age that he was a gentle soul. The kindest little boy you could have ever met. Nick was loved by everyone who ever had the pleasure of meeting him. He had the biggest heart, and he wore it right there on his sleeve. He cared about everyone and everything. It didn't matter if it was a turtle with a limp or a friend needing a place to stay, Nick would bring them home. Smaller children loved him because he always included them and made them feel validated, and the elderly loved him because he always spoke with the utmost respect to them. He was such a joy to be around.

Nicholas loved everything about the outdoors. Whether spear fishing in the coastal waterways, exploring quarries filled with alligators, skateboarding, or riding dirt bikes. He was always outdoors. When he was about five years old, we got him a dirt bike. He was so small that someone would have to hold him up when he was ready to take off, and when he was ready to stop, we would have to catch him when doing a drive-by. He eventually grew into his bike, and when he would outgrow that one, we would get him another. I even bought myself one so we could enjoy riding together.

We spent countless hours together riding trails. Occasionally, he would surprise me by veering off the road and into a ditch, so he could become airborne enough to jump completely over people's driveways. I was always in awe of how well he rode that dirt bike. He taught himself so many tricks and could ride a wheelie for miles. His love for riding on two wheels began at an early age and continued throughout his life. When he asked for a street bike for his graduation gift as his way of transportation, I wasn't surprised. However, I was against the idea because Florida has so many people on the roads, especially during the winter season when all the snowbirds (people from up north) come to stay.

But there's something about your child continuously asking for something you know they deserve, that wears you down. He had such a way with words . . . and those eyes. Every time I would attempt to sway him away from the street bike, he would gently remind me how many hours he had spent on those dirt bikes. I was so immensely proud of him and just wanted to give him what *he* wanted, and what I knew he deserved. He was so talented on that bike. Rick and I wanted him to be prepared, so we enrolled him in two separate state-approved motorcycle classes. Of course, he completed them both with flying colors, and we bought the bike. He was so proud of that bike. He would clean it, tune it, and turn some wrenches. Heck, he would even talk to her. He loved her so much that he gave her a name, Chloe. I'm sure those next seven months were the best he had ever got to experience.

By this time, Thanksgiving was coming up and we had planned on making the 18 hour trip to Ashlee's house. We were intending to leave the upcoming Friday and wanted Nick to be home on Thursday, so we could be all packed up and ready to hit the road. Nick had been staying and working with my nephew Brandon, who owns his own business. Nick wasn't feeling well that day, but came home anyway to surprise his momma, since he knew my birthday was the following day. His dad and I tried to talk him into staying with us that night, but Nicholas knew there was a job that needed to be done and insisted on returning to Brandon's house to fulfill his obligation. Looking back, I'm so glad he decided to come surprise me that day. Though it would become the worst day of my life, I am so very grateful that I was able to hug his neck, tell him and also hear for myself the words, "I Love You." There's just something about an embrace from your child—no one and nothing else can compare. I had no idea this would be the last time.

The accident that night changed my entire world in an instant and nothing would ever be the same. Brandon called me to inform me that Nick had not made it home yet and asked if I had spoken to him. I replied, "no." I was anticipating his call letting me know when he got there. We pinged the location of Nick's phone, and it showed he was about five miles from his destination, but the ping was now stationary. We both agreed that Brandon would drive to the location to check it out. He called me a few moments later to tell me that he saw a lot of police lights but did not see any motorcycle. He said it looked like there was indeed an accident, but he couldn't get any closer to confirm if it was Nick or not.

Rick and I ran to our car immediately and started the hour-and-a-half drive to the location. I began calling and texting Nick's phone, though there would not be an answer. I began calling every hospital within a 100-mile radius of the crash site begging them to tell me if there had been a motorcycle driver admitted from a crash. None of them had any motorcycle patients. This is when my world started to shatter. As we continued driving, I began praying, begging, pleading with God to not let this be happening.

After what felt like an eternity, we were approaching a roadblock that was approximately a half mile before the intersection of El Jobean Rd. and Cornelius Blvd., where Nick's phone was being pinged and police were detouring traffic. We tried to take a different route and encountered yet another roadblock. However, this time I got out of my vehicle and approached the police officer. I asked him if the reason for the roadblock was due to a motorcycle accident, and if so, it was my son and I wanted through. He didn't give me a clear answer but refused to let me and Rick through the roadblock and instead told us we needed to go to our nephew's home, and someone would come find us.

We drove to Brandon's home and began to wait. As we were waiting, my sister and her husband arrived, Nick's girlfriend Bella arrived, and I tried to keep myself busy by talking to Ashlee, who was 1,200 miles away. We waited for what felt like days. Just when I thought I couldn't wait any longer, we noticed headlights were coming down the road toward us. The closer they got, the more I began to see it was, in fact, a police car.

As he pulled into the driveway, I ran over to greet him, and he responded by asking for the parents of Nicholas Novak. Rick and I both spoke up, stating that we were in fact, Nick's parents. The moments following this were so surreal. With cold dead eyes, this cop looked at Rick and I and said, "There was an accident and Nicholas did not make it. There were witnesses that stated he was traveling at a high rate of speed and someone driving another vehicle thought they had enough time to cross the highway." His words were as cold as his eyes. Those words ended my life; they ended everything that I ever envisioned for myself, for my son, and for the generation to follow. My husband was an only child, so Nicholas was the one left to carry on the name. Everything died there that night with him.

Nick would always tell me things about street bikes when he was riding shotgun in my car. "Be sure to use your blinker Mom. Bikes come up beside you fast, so if you don't use a blinker, they may run into you." When I saw another motorcycle weaving in and out of traffic, I told him that he better not be doing that. He replied with, "Mom, we do that only to get into first position, because drivers can't see you if you're coming up beside them, but they can always see you when you're in front of them." So that is exactly what Nicholas was doing, trying to get into first position, trying to be seen, dying to be seen. In the weeks following the accident, there was an official investigation completed by a motorcycle speed specialist, in which they determined his speed to be 59 mph at the point of impact. This was a highway with a posted speed limit of 70 mph. The length of the skid mark made by Nick's bike was only 20 feet.

One of the witnesses to the accident reached out to me, to try and put the pieces together and to assure me that Nick did not feel any pain. He described the crash to us in detail. Through this, we learned Nick's bike disintegrated upon impact, and he flew about 20 feet into the air. The impact removed his helmet, his gloves, and even his shoes. All those years of riding motorcycles, those state approved riding classes, all the protective gear in the world couldn't protect him from hitting a full-size Dodge diesel 4x4 pickup truck. My baby was killed on impact.

Richie, our witness, then told us how he ran over to our son and stood over him so no other vehicles would run over him, and I am so grateful. He described how unbothered the man who killed Nicholas seemed to be. This elderly man admitted to the police, "Yea, I saw him coming but thought I had enough time to turn in front of him." The man was not injured and walked completely around Nicholas' lifeless body to be checked out by the ambulance. He didn't go to the hospital because he was not injured. Although he caused the accident, he didn't even get a ticket for *failure to yield*. To this day, we haven't heard one word from this man or anyone who knows him. I spent so much time being angry, so angry, that this man was not being held accountable for killing my child. It's hard to forgive someone who isn't sorry.

I won't lie. It took me a really long time to stop being mad, not only with that man, but with all elderly drivers that I saw on the road. I realized I could not condemn the entire world for the actions of one careless man.

I am now three years into this journey, and looking back, I can see where God was preparing me for this. There had been a few things that had happened to me over the course of my own life, as well as Nick's life. One of those things happened only three months before his fatal accident and on that day, he decided he wanted me to cut his hair. As I began to trim it, he said, "I don't feel too good," and, suddenly, he went limp and began to fall off of the bar stool. I grabbed his shoulders and we both fell to the floor, he stopped breathing and his lips began turning blue. I screamed for Rick while I shook Nicholas and yelled his name. Rick ran to us and started hitting Nick's chest, after the second blow he opened his eyes and gasped for air, bewildered, as to how he got in that current situation. We never learned why that particular event happened. Looking back now, I feel it was to show me that there was nothing I could have done to save Nick. He could have died there at home for no reason at all, and I cannot blame myself for him coming home that day.

That wasn't the only precursor. When I was a teenager, I had another profound thing happen to me. Something I believe was sent to me for comfort. I had an unfortunate accident while riding an ATV and ended up having an out-of-body experience. During the early morning hours, while it was still dark outside, several of us decided to take the ATVs out for a ride. We went into the woods, which were filled with large hills. As we began to climb a very large hill, the ATV started to bog down, and the front tires lifted off the ground. Rick hit the back break, and the front tires came back down and bounced. The force was so great that it threw Rick off the bike and left me on the back.

Then, the bike started traveling backward down the hill. In the black of night, as the headlights pointed straight up into the sky, suddenly, I was outside of my body. Standing at the top of the hill, watching myself ride down that hill on the bike. At the time, I was so scared by what had happened that I just wanted to go home and not talk about it. That experience was so profound, and to this day, I can remember the exact details of the entire event like it happened yesterday. Now I know why that happened to me all those years ago; it was to prepare me for this very time in my life. I feel it was God showing me Nicholas did not feel anything. Just as I was outside of my body during the four-wheeler incident, I know that Nicholas was outside of his body during his accident.

From the very beginning of this horrific tragedy, we have received so many undeniable, supernatural signs from Nicholas. We know without a doubt that he is still around trying to communicate with us the best he can. A few days after the accident, Nick's grandmother opened her bible to do her daily reading. That particular day, she was set to read from the Bible, Acts 6. As she turned the pages to Acts, she found a bookmark that Nick had made in the second grade and written on it was that very chapter— Acts 6:1-7. She thought, what a coincidence that her scheduled reading for the day was that very scripture. The subtitle for that chapter was, "Seven Chosen to Serve." As she began to read, she got to verse five and realized this was no coincidence and that this was Nicholas speaking to her. That verse lists the names of the seven people chosen to serve, to be appointed over God's business. One of those names is *Nicolas*. This is the only time that Nicholas is mentioned throughout the entire bible. I was in utter disbelief, but I was so engulfed in my grief that I couldn't see the true meaning of this until much later. I was caught in a whirlwind of denial and despair.

Two weeks had passed since the funeral and the fog of utter devastation and disbelief was still so thick. Rick and I were sitting in the garage talking and crying. The garage was our hangout of sorts with Nick. We loved to go out there and listen to the stereo while Nick worked on his bike, discussing the day or reminiscing on good times past. Next to the door that we would walk past every day, sat an old box, and I just had this strong urge to open it. I already knew what was inside the box, it was seven years of extra school supplies that we had accumulated. Every year we would have left-over supplies, and they would get placed into this one box. This box has literally gone through four different moves within those seven years.

I reached into the box and pulled out a handful of empty manila folders, and out with it, a red envelope fell to the floor. When I looked down, I saw Nick's handwriting on the envelope. It read, "I'm really sorry."

Eyes wide open, I looked up at Rick to make sure he was seeing what I was seeing, and of course, he was. I reached down to grab it and realized it was an envelope that Nick had given me with a Mother's Day card in 2010. The blessing was not what was made in that card seven years prior; the blessing was the message on the envelope all these years later—the envelope that *just so happened* to fall out of nowhere as I was wailing in my grief.

The message was as follows, *To momy from Nicholas & Nicholas only!!! Love u bye now open the card!* and on the other side, *I'm really sorry!!!* I must have read those words a hundred times, and each time I read them, I literally felt them.

It was as if Nicholas had his arms wrapped around me, and I could feel the warmth of his embrace; it was a true heavenly hug. It was only then that I remembered back to what Nick's grandmother told me about Nick being chosen to serve. I realized then unexplainable divine things were happening to and around us. These are the things that get me through each day—these and, of course, my beliefs in God and the afterlife. There is no way I could have made it this far without my faith. I believe the word of God is true, and I will see Nick again when it's my time to cross the veil to the other side.

It has been a little over three years, and it seems everything about me has changed. I am a completely different person now. Grief changes you, especially when grieving your child. As we age, we already know that death will eventually happen. We anticipate these events and somewhat prepare our hearts for it, but when you lose your child, the grief changes every fiber of your being. Losing my child took me to places I never knew really existed. As the days, weeks, and months continued without him, I became so angry. I just couldn't grasp that the world continued to go on, yet my world was completely broken and shattered. I was in the deepest, darkest hole with no way out.

Even though so many others have experienced this same horrific tragedy, I felt as if I was all alone, and no one knew what or how I was feeling. I started to totally isolate myself. I wanted to stay in my bed and never leave. I didn't care to see or speak to anyone. I felt like people were tired of hearing me say the same thing over and over, which was my reality. My child is gone, and for the rest of my life, I will never get to see or hold him again. I will never get the chance to see him get married or become the wonderful father I know he would've been. I was so angry that I just stopped caring. I stopped caring about life, nothing mattered to me anymore. Obviously, I still loved Rick, Ashlee, and my grandchildren, but everything else that mattered to others was obsolete. To hear people in conversation talking about mundane things enraged me.

After some time, I began to look at myself as ugly. You know, like when you're walking past someone and smile and they give you the ugliest look instead of smiling or saying, *hello* back. The person where you say to yourself, *man, she was a rude old woman.* Yea, that's who I had become. It took me awhile to realize it was not the world's fault that one irresponsible man made a poor decision, which altered my entire world. I didn't want to give Satan the pleasure of watching me destroy myself and everyone else around me. The word of God says that Satan comes to steal, kill, and destroy. I refuse to let him destroy me. It was at this time I decided to get as *even* with Satan as I could, and I started talking to everyone about God, trying to win as many souls as I could. I felt like this alone was punching him in the face every time someone would turn their life to Christ. I began to read the word of God, allowing him to work in me, not removing the pain, but seeing me through it.

I have learned through the many supernatural experiences that Nicholas can, in fact, communicate with us, but in a way we cannot completely understand. One day, not long after the funeral, I was in my backyard walking the dogs, and I audibly heard Nicholas scream as loud as he could. In a long-drawn-out tone I heard, "MOOOOOM!" and being so distraught, I thought, I am going crazy. Then again, a second time, the same thing, "MOOOOOM!" in a tone like when you're trying to get someone's attention from a distance. As soon as the last shout was over, I heard a female with a soft voice politely say, "She can't hear you." To this day, I can still remember, hear, and feel, the tones of both Nicholas's voice and the girl's voice.

That experience, that supernatural sign, is one thing that helps me get through each day. I firmly believe God allowed me to hear that, to show me my son is still able to see me. I can't see him, but he is there, he can see me. The signs from loved ones who have passed are all around us, but sometimes we are so distracted we miss them. Whether we are distracted by the daily grind or by grief itself, it's easy to miss the signs.

Personally, I have found social media groups for bereaved parents, such as Helping Parents Heal, to express my feelings without judgement. During this nightmare journey, your feelings will be all over the place. You will start to feel as though the ones who you love the most start to shy away from you because they are either tired of hearing about your pain and misery or they feel you should have "gotten over it" by now. Helping Parents Heal, along with other bereaved groups, gives you the opportunity to express yourself without judgement; to connect with like-minded people with the same broken heart. Through these groups, you will start to develop friendships that you had no idea would even transpire. In fact, this is exactly how I connected with Elly to even share my story with you, which I am ever so grateful for. Only the broken heart and soul of another grieving momma or daddy will know how you feel and can help along the way.

Losing my child has changed me to the very core. I know what complete darkness feels like. The hole that darkness resides in is very deep. In fact, I am still climbing out of it, but I *am* climbing out. It is possible. Nicholas had one tattoo on his arm which read, Philippians 4:13, *I can do all things through Christ who strengthens me.* Both Rick and I now have an exact replica, and in the same place that Nick had his, to remind us that we can do it.

I've also learned what not to do: do not sell your home, move, quit your job, or make any major change for at least two years. WAIT. I know this because I did all of them, and I regret all of them. The first two years are a complete blur to me; I was on complete auto pilot. I only remember bits and pieces because my mind and heart were scattered from here to Heaven. I've learned to take each day as it comes. There is no right or wrong. Our feelings are our feelings. When you have so much love to give, yet the person whom you want to share it with is not within your reach, it can sometimes knock you down. Just talk to them out loud, and then look for the signs.

Grief comes in waves. It will feel like you can't breathe when it washes over you. Just know that those feelings will pass even though others are sure to follow. Have your feelings and try not to stuff them down, and don't listen to anyone who says, "You have to move on." This isn't something you can just move on or recover from. This is something you absorb into your new reality.

Angela Novak, Nicholas's Mom

Angela Novak is a southern girl, having grown up in a Louisiana town, where eating mudbugs and having Mardi Gras parades is a given. Whether a national holiday, town festival, or any given Sunday, you can find Angela surrounded by a multitude of family members. With Sicilian blood in her veins, you know where her love stems from: faith, family, and food. She was born into a large loving Italian family, where weekly Sunday dinner gatherings at Grandma's house are a normal way of life. It was a place where love and family values were learned and later cherished.

She married her high-school sweetheart right out of school and within a year started a family. In 2006, she moved the family to Florida for better opportunities. She was living a fairytale dream until her world shattered in November of 2017, when she became a mom to an angel. She is now a bereaved mom obsessed with everything afterlife. Learning to navigate between the spiritual world and the physical world has become her new normal. Angela attributes her healing progress to learning about the afterlife and opening her mind and eyes to the signs placed before her. She takes each day as it comes; knowing one more day without her son also means it's one day closer to seeing him in paradise.

#checktwicesavealife

#bikerslivesmatter

#nicknovakforever19

If you would like to reach out to Angela, her email is Angela.novak@icloud.com

AMANDA

Watching over Her Angels

My husband and I met when we were in junior high school. We got married young and had four beautiful children. We have three sons: Michael, Mark, and Daniel. Our youngest is our beautiful daughter Amanda Michelle. My nickname for her is Bugz. She is my Amanda Bugz. Amanda was born on May 3, 1996, just under five pounds. She was tiny and could fit inside the palm of your hand. She had a little bit of a rough start but fought her way through it. After a week of being in the hospital, she finally came home to meet her brothers. Once home, we went through weeks of crying, changing formulas, and sleepless nights before we found out she had acid reflux, but once treated, she was a happy baby. The first 18 months were a lot of ups and downs for her. Amanda ended up contracting respiratory syncytial virus (RSV) and had a milk allergy. She was not able to drink milk until she was almost two years old and hated to drink it later in life. Amanda was a fighter through it all.

Amanda also suffered from anxiety separation her whole young life. It is a daily struggle. Simple little things like going to school, being around people she did not know, being left alone, or even something as simple as checking the mail could trigger an event. She would go over to friends' houses for sleepovers, and when it was time to go to sleep, her dad or I would have to pick her up.

Amanda, from a young age, loved cheerleading and dance. Her dad and I took her for tumbling lessons, and in third grade, she tried out for pee-wee cheerleading at her school and made the team. She was so excited. She cheered for her school and joined another competitive squad. She wanted to help coach girls on a squad and teach them that it is not always about winning. She wanted them to learn and have fun while doing it.

Amanda also had a love for animals. If I would let her, she would have brought all the stray animals home. She wanted a midget dog, so for Christmas one year, we got her a Yorkie, and she named her Midget. She was her best friend throughout most of her life. Amanda would paint her nails, dress her up, and put her in her baby doll stroller. Midget would just sit there too. Amanda told me she wanted to be a veterinarian and help all the animals. She had one hamster, two guinea pigs, and three dogs. We still have two of the dogs: a teacup Chihuahua named Badger and a beagle named Luna.

Amanda was always a very determined child. If someone told her she could not do something, she would prove them wrong. Her senior year of high school, she got pregnant, and a few people told her she would not graduate. Some kids even poked fun at her; however, we told her to walk proudly through the school halls and keep her chin high. She did just that.

Later that year, she walked proudly for her diploma just two months after giving birth to her son, Isaiah. She said graduating was one of her greatest accomplishments due to the challenges of being pregnant in high school. She wanted to continue schooling after graduation and study criminal justice, but her relationship with Isaiah's father ended, and it broke her for some time. Amanda was always a pleaser, even if it did not make her happy.

My relationship with my baby girl was special. She was my world and my best friend. We were always together and loved taking day trips to malls in different parts of town, where we would shop and have lunch together. We would plan our family vacations—there had to be water and shopping involved—and her dad was just along for the ride. He secretly did not mind. Amanda and I would sit down and watch television shows and movies together: the "lovesick ones" as her dad called them. There was never a time we did not know what the other was doing. Even when she moved out with her boyfriend, she was at our house more than her house, or she would call me to come over there. I deeply miss those days, and I would not change them for the world. I wish we had done even more together if that was possible.

When Isaiah was about 10 months old, Amanda met a guy, Matt, from where she was working at the time. He was a police officer at a local municipality. She brought him to the house for me to meet. Her dad already knew him and his father, who was chief of police in an area near our community. I thought she finally met a nice guy, but after he left our house for their date, I walked into the living room and told my husband there was something about him I did not like. Mark said for me to give him a chance because our daughter seemed happy. I kind of mumbled and said I would try. They continued to date, but at one point, they broke up, and he found another girlfriend. I was not surprised. A few weeks later, they got back together, and he seemed to be doing good by her. They took a few small vacations here and there. He would take her and Isaiah to special places as a family. I was starting to like him. I did let him know a few different times that she was my baby girl and Isaiah was my grandbaby, so he better not hurt them. He would say he understood, but I knew he had no clue.

There was a point when Matt was having problems at home with his family, and Amanda asked if he could move in with us for a little while—just until he worked things out at home or until he found a place to move. He ended up living with us until they got their own place. Amanda soon became pregnant again with her second son, Rowan. We were told she had to get pregnant, or he was going to leave her. Amanda and Matt moved into their apartment, which was about two miles from our house. They moved the end of June, and it was heart breaking for us—our baby was leaving. Amanda cried a lot too. I told her if she did not want to move, she did not have to, but she wanted to make her little family work.

After they moved, Matt was hired as a deputy sheriff and still worked part-time as a police officer. He never seemed to be around. I used to tell her no one works that much, but she did not want to believe he was doing anything wrong. Amanda worked for Verizon and loved her job, but she needed help with Isaiah, so I cut my hours back at my job and helped take care of him. Amanda did not trust many people with her son.

Amanda and Matt's relationship was rocky at times. He never wanted much to do with family gatherings. He never wanted to go away on our little trips. We liked to take weekend getaways to the beach or go watch our one granddaughter cheer at competitions. He would fight with Amanda every time we went away or accuse her of having another guy around. Sometimes she would block him on her phone so he could not bother her. He never wanted anyone else around, so they would occasionally take their own trips.

Amanda went on maternity leave about three weeks before Rowan was born. We spent a lot of time together. I spent much of my time helping her clean up her house cleaned and getting the baby's stuff cleaned and put away. Even Isaiah helped me put furniture together for his baby brother. He was so excited for his brother to arrive. Amanda and Matt seemed to be doing well. They were all excited for Rowan's arrival.

After Rowan was born, Amanda went back to work, which was about two weeks later. She was required to make a certain percentage each month to keep her job, and after returning to work so quickly, she was not able to reach the required percentage, so she was let go. This started to hurt Amanda and Matt's relationship. He said he could not afford to keep it all going. She never knew what he made or brought home each month because they had separate bank accounts. Matt even messaged her boss and proceeded to tell her what he thought of her, and it was not a nice message.

Amanda just did not seem herself after Rowan was born. She was always moody and short with everyone. I thought she was suffering from post-partem depression. I was always asking her if she was ok, and she would say she was fine, with an attitude. A couple of times, I found black and blue marks on her and when I would ask her what had happened, she would say she fell or slipped out of bed. Amanda was not a klutz, but I did not push the issue.

Things with Matt and I were not going well, and he seemed to be putting a wedge between Amanda and me. He was the cause of a big argument between us because I told her not to waste her money. He told Amanda that I should just drop her off at their house and not come in, or he was going to tell me off. Amanda and I did not talk for a few days. Then he brought home a dog for her. I was mad at her because I knew I would be the one taking care of it. He would do little things like that knowing we would have words.

Amanda got a job in sales, but she hated it. She decided to keep it until she was able to find another one, and also come back to work with me until she could get back on her feet. Then she landed a job at Staples. She loved that, and they loved her too. She seemed to be coming, somewhat, back to herself. She continued to work two jobs and get caught up on her bills. She enjoyed doing things with her boys on her days off, like going for walks around her little community. Amanda was planning for her oldest son's third birthday, and for those who did not know Amanda, she always went way out for her boys. In her eyes, they would always be first. The theme for his birthday was construction workers. She enjoyed ordering his outfit and party supplies, and we went all over the place to make his party special. I told her she should think about becoming a party planner.

Matt and his parents were invited to Isaiah's party, but it still shocked me when they showed up. The party went very well until the end when Matt's parents became upset and left the party. I am a baby hog, so I thought they were mad because I did not let them hold Rowan much. I found out later that night that Matt and his parents got into a disagreement over visiting with the baby. Matt told us his dad made some cruel remarks about how he would bash Matt's skull in. This took place while they were at Isaiah's party—totally unacceptable!

It was not the first time I had heard about stuff like this. Amanda was upset over what was said to Matt. She asked how someone could be that mean to their child, especially because Matt's dad was a chief of police. Amanda said he deals with people who act just like that all the time. Matt was going to move to get away from his dad after what he said and years of being treated unfairly. I felt like Matt was always seeking approval from his father, so he tried to be like him. He became a police officer like him, even after making it clear it was not what he desired, trying to please his dad and maybe gain his acceptance.

Isaiah had a visit with his dad the weekend of his birthday, which was also Easter. Amanda made an Easter basket for the boys, and one for her big kid Matt. She cooked Easter dinner and invited us over after Isaiah got home so we could have cake and ice cream for his actual birthday. Matt worked so we did not see him at all that day. Some days that was a relief for me—I did not have to be on guard. I helped her clean up and get the boys ready for bed before we left. Isaiah always wanted me to stay and sleepover with him. Little did I know that would be my last holiday with Amanda and the last one she would spend with her boys.

The next eight days seemed to be normal for them. I did not hear much about them having problems. We started to plan Amanda's twenty-first birthday, which was coming up fast. Matt was even involved in the planning. Amanda wanted to go to the casino because she loved to gamble and was usually lucky. We had planned to go to a casino about an hour away and make it a weekend celebration. We wanted to make it special for her because she was always thinking of others and making them feel special. She was super excited about going and said maybe she would hit the jackpot.

April 24, 2017, was like any other day. Amanda came to work to relieve me from my shift, and I took Isaiah and went home. Matt was working at the sheriff's department, and then I believe was putting signs out for the upcoming election. Amanda was in a good mood at work. I made supper and took some to her and her coworker. Matt had been texting me throughout the night asking questions about her birthday getaway. Later that night, Amanda called me and asked if I would watch the boys in the morning because her other job had called her in, and I said "yes." I told her they could just spend the night, so she did not have to wake them up early to bring them to our house.

Amanda got off work at 10 p.m. that night and stopped by the house to see the boys before she went home and help me get them ready for bed. Amanda picked Rowan up, kissed him, and said, "I love you Mommy's little fatty." Then she went into the bathroom and kissed Isaiah. She told him to be good for Maw Maw and Pappy. She told him if he was a good boy, they would go to the store after she got off work. When Amanda was done loving on the boys, she came back to the living room and kissed her dad and I before she left for her house. I told her to let me know when she got home so I did not worry. I got the boys settled in bed for the night and was on my way to bed.

I got a phone call from her at 11:51 p.m. telling me she needed her dad to come for her because Matt would not let her leave. I asked her what was going on and she said he had been drinking with a few coworkers, and one of the coworkers said something that upset Matt. I asked her what was said, and she told me she would explain when she got home. I told her to please bring clothes for the baby. While she was walking up the steps to grab clothes, Matt was walking up behind her yelling and wanting to know who she was on the phone with and she said, "My mother and my dad is coming for me." He said, "What is he going do?" and she said, "You will see when he gets here." A few seconds later her phone went dead. I thought she hung up on me. I yelled at her dad to go get her and see what is going on. Little did I know that was the last conversation I would have with her.

Mark had left to drive over to their apartment. We were only about five minutes from their house. I kept calling Amanda's phone and my husband's phone over and over and no one would answer. I knew in my gut something was not right. I called my son who lived next door to me and told him briefly what was going on. I told him no one was answering my calls and asked him to go see what was going on? It seemed like he was taking too long, so I called him again, and he said, "Mum, I am hurrying, but I am following an ambulance."

I hung up. I knew it was not good. It felt like two seconds, and my son was in my house. His dad had called him and told him what had happened, and he explained it to me when he got to my house.

He said, "Mum, listen please."

I said, "He hurt my daughter."

My son kept saying, "You must calm down, the boys are here." He said, "She is gone." and I lost it.

I said, "Please take me to their apartment." He told me "No" and that I needed to be here with the boys. I kept begging *please*. I finally had my mother drive me over to their apartment.

I jumped out of my mother's car and ran to the apartment and begged for them to let me in, "My husband is in there. Please let me in to see my baby!"

The officer said he could not do that. I asked him if he had any daughters, he replied, "Yes."

I said, "How would you feel if that was your daughter in there?" and "I just wanted to hold my baby, please."

The officer said he still could not let me in.

I do not remember too much after that. I was told I was yelling at the officers and other people around and crying. I do not even remember how I got back to my house. I just remember being in my driveway and crying with all my family and friends around asking, "WHY?!" My baby girl— my mini, my best friend, and my world—was shot in the back of her head by her boyfriend. I was told she did not suffer so that gave me a little peace. Then her boyfriend shot himself. He was still breathing when my husband got there, so Mark called 911 to get him help. He did not make it. He died at the hospital. I called his mother and said a few mean things to her—a big part of me died that night too— and I knew the stress ahead of us. We had a long week coming with having to plan her funeral and buy a burial plot. Knowing I had to tell Amanda's oldest son that his mommy is in heaven and not coming back home to us was so very heartbreaking.

The viewing was very emotional for me. I could not go up and look at her lying there. There were so many people and trying to keep it all together was tough for me. Her service was beautiful. The next day we laid her to rest, which was the day before her 21st birthday. I felt like I was in a fog, and I would wake up from this nightmare. I walked up to the casket with my boys and husband to say our goodbyes. My heart broke when they closed the casket. I knew from that moment on life would never be the same for me. The next day, which was her birthday, we went and released balloons for her.

Life after Amanda's death has left an unimaginable void in all our lives. The grieving was tough to handle. I wanted to be dead too and had thoughts about suicide. I started drinking heavily and putting blame on people who did not deserve it. My marriage was falling apart, and we separated for a few months. Amanda's oldest son was taken away from me by his father, and I was not allowed to see him. I was devastated.

Amanda's youngest son was all I felt I had left. He was the only reason I had for getting out of bed each day and trying to function. Poor baby had no clue what was going on in the world around him. I believe he is my saving grace. I tell everyone he loved me through all the ugliness that was going on. I finally had to seek professional counseling, I felt I could not talk to someone who had no clue how I was feeling. How could they understand me and what I was going through?

I did a group session with families that had lost loved ones to violence. That was a big help to me; after that, I started one-on-one counseling. I felt I was finally letting out some of my pain, not all of it, but enough that I was feeling relief. I have a hard time opening up to people and letting them see the vulnerable side of me. I still blame myself for not seeing the signs; 1 too lived with domestic violence when I was young. I was lucky and I was able to get out. I wanted to know why she felt she could not talk to me about what was going on in her private life. I would have moved the world for her, to keep her and her boys safe. Everyone thinks she did not tell me things because she knew how I felt about him, and she did not want to add anything that would make it worse.

I do not think you ever stop grieving. I think you move forward on a different journey as a different person who does not take life for granted. Little things in life have a different value to you than they do for other people. I always say this to *normal* people because when you lose a child nothing in life is normal anymore.

I was left with two big parts of Amanda's life: her two boys. Her oldest, I have guardianship of, and he is happily living with us after a few months of court battles. He is thriving in school and in sports. Her youngest, we have temporary guardianship of, and he is still in our home. He is in preschool and doing well also. He cannot wait to go to school with his big brother; it is all he talks about. My husband and I will keep battling as long as it takes and do whatever is necessary to keep them together. These boys help us to keep her memory alive. Together, they can take on whatever life throws their way. They both have parts of their mom in them in different ways. They love to go up to the cemetery and decorate her resting spot for the different holidays. I just pray their bond is never broken.

We keep Amanda's memory alive by helping others with domestic violence. My husband, the boys, and I do whatever we can for our local women's center, including taking the boys down to visit and raising money for the shelter. I want to teach them that violence does not solve problems. I want them to see how the ugliness can affect other people. I want them to be a positive change in the world for everyone, everywhere. We also have an annual bike run and basket party in her honor, and we plan to offer a scholarship at her high school. Amanda loved animals, so I have plans to help our local animal shelter. I also want to be able to help a family with legal counsel in a domestic violence situation, but we are working on becoming a nonprofit first. I want her boys to carry on with all that we do in her honor when they are older.

I am moving forward in a different form of life as a mother of a child who was taken way too soon. I have become guarded. I have learned to trust my instincts more, and I do not take much for granted. I realize that life can be short. I still have questions as to why . . . why my baby, my only girl, why any of our children? How could someone be that heartless and take a life? How could he take her away from her boys and leave one motherless and the other one an orphan? He left two families fighting court battles to gain guardianship of a little boy. I just want the boys kept together, because at the end of the day, they are all they have left and being brothers could help them grow and heal together. After the court battles pass and the boys are grown—which really does pass quickly—they have their whole lives to remember, to heal, and to be the best they can despite their early years. I pray that they will always stay close and not let what happened to them tear them apart. These two boys keep me moving forward. My husband and I now play the role as their parents and yet still try to be their grandparents also.

On my really bad days, I just sit and talk to our daughter, whether it is to a picture of her or a visit to the cemetery. I tell her how much I miss and love her; I tell her all about her big boys and about their journeys at the time. I always ask if I am making her proud and doing well with her boys—the way she would have wanted them to be raised. I find peace when I can visit her almost as if she is sitting right beside me, talking to me. I am always looking to see signs of her in everything I do and all the places I go. She loved to travel. I just imagine what she would be saying or doing, especially with the boys. There are nights I still cry myself to sleep from missing her so much.

In this new journey, I need to take it moment by moment instead of day by day.

As you learn to move forward, you must let go of holding their hand, talking face-to-face, and not having them by your side. Although this ugly, painful reality will never truly go away, the days and nights will begin to pass with less breakdowns and tears and fewer thoughts running wild in your mind. Do not beat yourself up for feeling less pain over time, you are simply learning to coexist with the hurt.

I was told that sometimes your heart needs more time to accept what your mind already knows. Some say God never gives you more than you can handle; He must think we are amazing mothers. Always remember that no matter where you are in life, no matter what you are doing, or who is around, you can speak freely to your child. It does not always have to be under your breath or in your mind's eye. Let your child hear your voice out loud, just as they always have and always will.

I continue my relationship with my daughter only in a different manner. Many people say, *try to let go, try to move on*, *do not think so much*, but you will never be able to do that. This reality is part of who you are now, sewn into your very fabric, your very being. As a parent, I will never let go or forget; Amanda remains a daily part of my life. Silence is what brought my family to where we are today, and since that day, the silence has ended.

E Michelle Bennett, Amanda's Mom

Ellison Reba Michelle Bennett, known as simply Michelle, was born July 26, 1967, in Johnstown Pa., where she has lived most of her life. She graduated in 1985 from Mt. Lebanon High School in Pittsburgh, Pa.. She married her husband, Mark, in 1988 and has four children: Michael, Mark, Daniel, and Amanda. She has worked most of her life in retail and the better part of that as a manager of a mom-and-pop store and sub shop. Since losing her daughter in 2017, she has been a stay-at-home grandma raising her daughter's two sons, Isaiah and Rowan. She also helps with all her other grandchildren— and she has a lot. She and her husband plan to move south at some point in their later years because she loves to be near the beach and water.

Michelle works hard to raise awareness about domestic violence and helps with the local women's help center. Michelle and her husband hold an annual fundraiser in their daughter's honor and donate to their local shelter. It is called Amanda's Angel Run, and you can find out more information by visiting her Facebook page at www.facebook.com/BUGZ5396.

Email: michelle_bennett27@yahoo.com

COLIN

You Are My Sunshine

Colin Vincent Montesano joined my husband, Mike, and I on February 11, 1996, and made us a family. He was born three weeks early, but little did we know at that time, he would complete many of his milestones earlier than most kids.

He had a full head of black hair and was one of the cutest babies I have ever seen. He was the first grandchild on both sides of the family and was doted on by his grandparents, aunts, and uncles. He was a happy baby. We read and sang to him from the start, and he became a lover of books and music. I did everything to make and keep him healthy. I ate healthy during my pregnancy, nursed him for nine months, and never let anyone smoke in his presence. Despite this, he had a lot of ear infections, ended up with tubes, and needed speech therapy to be able to form his sounds correctly. This didn't hold him back though. He was talking and conversing at a very early age. Since we read so much, he was able to learn the sound of each letter and was reading independently at age four.

Colin loved sports at an early age. He played soccer, baseball, and hockey. He stuck with hockey from age six to 18. He decided that being a goalie was his passion, and he played for his high school team from eighth grade through his senior year.

Colin had a thirst for information. He wanted to know about everything. He would research whatever he was interested in at that moment, and he was an "A" student with what seemed like a photographic memory. He easily retained information he read or heard.

In 1998, when Colin was 2 and half years old, Evan joined our family. The boys were typical brothers who liked to pick on each other, wrestle, and goof around. They shared many of the same interests and became friends who hung out in the same circles, and their best friends were also brothers.

One of my favorite past times was as they got older, right before they went up to bed, I would go up to my room first, and listen to them laugh and giggle with each other. What I wanted most was for my boys and their families to be close long after my husband and I were gone.

Colin and I were close, especially when he was young. He looked to me to teach him what he was curious about by reading to him or talking about random things. He asked a lot of questions. I would lie on his bottom bunk with him at night, before he was ready to fall asleep, and we would read and talk for a long time. He also relied on me to cook all his favorite foods. He was a very adventurous eater. When he was in elementary school, he would order salmon, a rack of ribs, or alligator bites when we went out to dinner. He had no fear of trying new foods, and he also enjoyed oysters, bison burgers, and turtle soup as he got older. He always loved a good steak and hamburger, as well. As his mom, I enjoyed cooking for him because he always liked whatever I made. I also loved that he would come to me seeking advice when he was having girl problems or when he had an important decision to make.

Our family has always resided in Rochester, New York. In August 2014, Colin left home to attend the University of Pittsburgh (Pitt) where he studied biology. The day we left him behind in Pittsburgh was one of the hardest days of my life. I felt like I was abandoning my child. I adjusted pretty quickly over the next few weeks as I realized he loved it there, was doing well, and met a great group of friends. He was happy, which made me happy.

He was always interested in medicine, but it was at Pitt that he decided he wanted to apply to medical school and become a surgeon. He worked hard in his biology labs doing research on mice to eradicate the parasite *Toxoplasma gondii* which can be devastating to humans. He was earning "As" while also having fun with his friends.

In March of 2017, Colin came home for spring break for a week. When he went back to school to finish the semester, we made plans to go visit him the following month. When it came time to visit Colin a few weeks later, he had a busy weekend planned, so we decided to wait and visit him another time. We didn't want him to feel torn between spending time with us and the plans he had already made. Little did we know what was to come.

On Friday, April 21, 2017, I texted back and forth from work with Colin, to wish him well on his neurology exam. He texted when he was done, saying it was easy and he had finished quicker than he expected. This was the last day of classes for Colin. In a couple of days, he would be considered a college senior. He was in the homestretch and getting ready to study for his MCAT (Medical College Admission Test) exam.

That night, Mike, Evan— who had come home from his college for the weekend—and I ate a late dinner, and I decided to check in with Colin at 8:09 p.m. I sent him a celebration meme text and said, "I hope you are having a good time." I didn't hear back from him but didn't think anything of it. At 8:45 p.m., I got a call from Shane, one of his friends who also attended Pitt with him. Now, seeing his name and number come up on my phone on a Friday night was odd. I answered quickly, wondering what was wrong. Shane said there had been an accident and that Colin had fallen from a roof.

I started yelling to my husband and son Evan. They both came running to the room. Shane didn't have much information other than Colin was in surgery, and they were checking for a brain bleed and abdominal bleeding. My mind was racing. Do we get a flight to Pittsburgh? Do we leave in the morning and drive there? Isn't there a doctor that I can talk to for more information? Shane gave the phone to a Pitt police officer that was in the emergency department with a large group of Colin's friends. I remember asking him if we should come or wait until the morning. Were we talking about a couple of broken legs? We can manage and get through this, I thought.

The officer said to me, "You should come now. He's critical." That was all I needed to hear. We packed our car, asked a neighbor to watch our dog, and got on the road for the four-hour drive. Around 10 p.m., the social worker from the emergency department called us. She wanted to know what time we would be arriving. I told her we would be there between 2–2:30 a.m.

The drive was long, but we raced to get there. I texted with some friends and co-workers to let them know what was going on, and that I would be out of work for awhile, thinking Colin would need help with recuperation. My brother decided to leave work in Syracuse and meet us in Pittsburgh.

The social worker called several more times on the drive. She had no answers for me when I asked other than, "He is still in surgery." I asked to talk to the doctors, but they never called to give us any updates. This didn't feel right, and we suspected the social worker was keeping information from me and even shared those thoughts, which she never confirmed. She kept asking our ETA and my answer was always the same.

When I got a text from someone from the Pitt student affairs department, also asking our ETA, my suspicions grew.

We arrived at the entrance to University of Pittsburgh Medical Center's emergency department at 2:15 a.m. I remember seeing a group of 30 to 40 college students in the waiting room, some faces I recognized as Colin's closest friends and roommates. The staff had been waiting for us. They quickly led us to a room that had pamphlets about death, dying, and grief, and it was then that I knew what I had been suspecting the last few hours of the drive. The social worker went to get the trauma surgeon, and when he walked in, I said, "Did you bring us in here to tell us our son died?" He replied, "Yes, he did."

I was angry. I was angry that he didn't try hard enough to save my son's life. I was angry when they said his time of death was 10:04 p.m., which was before we even left Rochester. The surgeon rushed away to his next patient, and we talked to other doctors that were able to explain what happened and what efforts were made to try and save him. I went to the waiting room to tell Colin's friends the news, but all I could do was look into the crowd and shake my head *no*, and I quickly turned around and went back to the room where my husband and son were sobbing in disbelief and sadness.

The staff asked if we wanted to see Colin, and, of course, we did. The wait took forever. We invited his friends and my brother to come in with us. When we finally got to see him, he looked as if he was asleep. I think I expected to see a lot of facial injuries, considering how far he fell. We gathered around him, and a priest came to say a prayer. Then everyone left and the three of us spent some time alone with Colin. I took a photo of my hand clenching his; it's the last photo I have. I rubbed his hair and face. I sat there and looked at him, and I couldn't believe this was happening. The staff gave us his belongings. His cell phone that was in his pocket during the fall was intact, not a single crack. We got back to the hotel around 5 a.m. and got some sleep, until we got a call from the organ donation agency. Since the efforts to place him on life support were unsuccessful, we were not able to donate his vital organs, but they wanted to know if we wished to donate Colin's tissues, skin, and corneas. We knew that Colin had registered as an organ and tissue donor three months before he died, so we said "yes."

The next few days are a blur. The college had put us up in a hotel on Pitt's campus. It was really hard for us to be there. The weather was warm and sunny, and students were outside studying on the lawn, playing Frisbee, and enjoying the weekend before final exams started. We spent a couple of hours packing up Colin's room at his apartment. Colin's Pitt friends, Ian and Shane, were both from Rochester, and we had gotten to know their families well over the last few years. Their parents drove to Pitt to support us, and the boys, and were kind enough to take Colin's belongings back to Rochester for us. My sister and her husband arrived at Pitt, from New York City, the next day to be with us.

Colin's large group of friends planned a campus vigil and invited us to stay, but we felt we needed to get back to Rochester. Being at Pitt was difficult and we now had a funeral to plan. They were kind enough to send us a video of the entire vigil. Leaving Colin behind at the morgue in Pittsburgh was very difficult and so painful. The funeral home arranged to transport him back to Rochester the next day.

Over the course of the next few days, I learned more details of what happened. Colin and some of his friends had gone out to dinner and then headed back to Colin's apartment to play video games. After a while, Colin and his friend Matt, decided they wanted to get milkshakes. As they walked up to the main road, where all the restaurants and stores were, they passed some other friends who were hanging out on the roof of their apartment and invited them up. They continued on to get their milkshakes but went up on their way back. It was about 8:15 p.m. when they got there. This was only a few minutes after I had sent Colin the text that he never replied to. At 8:45 p.m., they decided to leave, and Colin went over to a couple people to say "goodbye." The music was on, and he was dancing around when he tripped over a pipe, or something, that was sticking up out of the floor of roof. This was a roof that they were not supposed to be on because there was no railing, only a 16-to-18-inch brick ledge. When Colin tripped, he fell backward over the ledge and down 25 feet to the concrete below. He had no broken arms or legs. He had a few broken ribs and a severe, fatal head injury. He had a pulse when he arrived at the hospital a few minutes later, but his brain damage was so severe, they weren't able to stabilize his oxygen levels. They rushed him to surgery where he died within the hour of his arrival to UPMC Hospital.

The weekend following his death, hundreds of people came through during calling hours to give us their condolences. Many people made the trip from Pittsburgh and some from even farther away. We celebrated Colin's life with a beautiful funeral, in which some of his closest friends and family shared memories of him. I was present, participated, socialized, and probably even smiled or laughed a time or two, but it was all just a formality. I was numb inside. When the hearse drove away to take Colin to the crematory, it was still unbelievable, and the pain of losing my boy was only just beginning.

Colin had been away at college for three years when he died. I was used to not seeing him or having his presence in our home daily. We texted every day and talked on occasion, sometimes more in depth and sometimes just a quick message to say, *Hope you had a good day. Stay safe. Make good choices. Love you.* I often feel that, because he had been away at school for so long, my reality didn't set in for a long time. Nights were very hard for the first several years. I cried myself to sleep every night until I was so exhausted that my eyes couldn't remain open. The house was quiet at night, and my brain would relive the trauma of him falling. Was he scared? Was he in pain? Did he know he was dying? Was he wondering where his mom was? It was my job to protect him, and I had such guilt that I wasn't able to. Survival after the sudden loss of a child is very hard, no matter the age of that child. It wasn't expected and I didn't get to thank him for making me a mom, tell him how much I loved him, and say "goodbye."

I had so much love and support from family and friends in the beginning, and it was still so hard. A meal train was organized so we had daily meals for a couple of months. We would have lived on cereal otherwise, so that was very helpful and appreciated. I learned early on to not make plans or commitments. I hate letting people down, and I didn't want to feel even worse if I had to cancel. I found, and still find to this day, that grief is inconsistent. My moods and emotions would change as quickly as the wind would change direction. I could feel ok one minute and be sobbing the next, with no specific reason or cause. I took some time off from work and tried to go back after about six weeks, but I couldn't concentrate and didn't feel like an effective employee, so I took more time off and went back part-time six months after losing Colin. I learned to take one day at a time and even one minute at a time. I learned to let myself stay in bed if I felt like that was what I needed. I didn't wear makeup for a long time because it irritated my eyes with all of the crying, and I have cried a lot of tears since that day.

Our other son, Evan, was 19 years old when we lost Colin. He is now 22. Losing his brother suddenly made both my husband and I constantly worried about something tragic happening to Evan and losing him, too. He is at an age where he is trying to become independent, and he's had to deal with two parents who are worried something bad is going to happen every time he walks out the door. He has handled that well and always sends a text before he drives, so we know when to expect him. He seems to understand our concerns and, thankfully, this has gotten easier for us over time.

Soon after Colin's death, I became connected with some mothers who also lost children. We get together often for coffee or a meal and text regularly to check on each other and offer support. Another local mom holds a luncheon a couple of times a year, which allows all of us to get together. Knowing there are others who understand me and that I am not alone is paramount to my grieving process.

When I was feeling sad and alone, I would write letters to Colin to get my feelings out. Sometimes, I was expressing anger at him for going on the roof and then dying and leaving us. Sometimes, I was expressing to him how much I love him and miss him and how sorry I felt I couldn't save him. We went to family grief counseling for a while, and I also saw a therapist individually. People are familiar with stages of grief, but in my experience, they don't occur in a specific order: they come and go, wax and wane, and then come back around again. What I do know is that the grief is still there and will always be, however, it is not as close to the surface as it used to be.

Six weeks after we lost Colin, we added a new puppy to the family. At first, I really didn't want the responsibility. I felt I could hardly take care of myself, let alone a puppy that requires a lot of training and dedication. I quickly became so attached to him and him to me. He is my little shadow, my snuggle partner, and brings me and my family so much needed joy. He was born exactly one month before Colin died, and we adopted him in June 2017. He just turned four, and I can't imagine my life without him. We named him Baxter after the dog in *Anchorman*, Colin's favorite movie. Colin and Baxter would have adored each other.

I read books and articles about grief and follow some grief groups on Facebook. One of those groups is Helping Parents Heal. Through this page, I have connected with other parents around the world. Each day, as I scroll through the HPH Facebook page, I see the faces of beautiful children that have gone too soon. I read posts from their grieving parents whose stories can be both heartbreaking and beautiful. Sometimes I feel compelled to leave a short message or a simple heart emoji to let them know that they are not alone. I enjoy the inspirational poems and quotes that people share on the page as they help me cope. On special occasions or on a particularly difficult day, I share a photo of Colin and read the inspiring messages left for me. I have found some interesting podcasts to follow to keep my mind occupied and busy. I listen to music often. Sometimes, I choose uplifting music to improve my mood, and sometimes I choose emotional music to express my grief and sadness.

When you lose a child suddenly, you get a glimpse of how quickly and easily life can change. The phrases *life is fragile* and *life is short* now make perfect sense. It makes you afraid and worried about losing others. You may even fixate on that fear, and it becomes draining and exhausting. You don't think you're going to survive the loss of your child, and then, somehow, you just do. You put one foot in front of the other and before you know it, days become weeks, and weeks become years. There is never a day that goes by that Colin isn't on my mind. I am able to take time out when I need it. I take alone time when I need space. Sometimes, I drive to the park, sit in my car, talk to Colin, and cry before I head back home. Often, it feels like a relief to get the feelings out.

The sadness is an underlying part of my new existence. It has taken a few years to get here, but I now understand that joy and sadness can be parallel in my life. I smile and laugh when I am with friends or family now, or if something strikes me as funny. I now welcome occasional joy when it used to make me feel guilty. I continue to work part-time so I have a sense of contributing to society and the family finances. I work in early intervention with children ages birth to three and their families, which is rewarding and brings a sense of accomplishment.

When you've lost a child, you long for signs from them to reassure you they are OK. The signs I receive come in the forms of music and cardinals. We had never seen a cardinal in our yard in the 10 years we lived in our home before Colin's death. We started to notice them on a regular basis ever since, and the sound of their singing brings us comfort.

Colin loved all kinds of music. There are times that we hear music that reminds us of him, and it comes at times that are too coincidental not be a sign. I met a friend for dinner one night and we talked and reminisced a lot about Colin. On the 15-minute drive home, I heard three songs on three different stations that rarely played on the radio anymore. I believe he was letting me know that he was with me and was trying to comfort me.

Because Colin had planned to attend medical school to become a surgeon, we decided to carry on his legacy by having a blood drive in his memory. The first blood drive was in 2017 and was such a huge success that we decided to hold one every year on the Saturday after Thanksgiving. In the fall of 2017, Colin's friends also held a blood drive on campus and collected 70 units of blood. We hold the annual blood drive at his high school, and it draws a lot of our local community. It's nice to see Colin's high school friends and college friends and their families. To date, we have had over 513 blood donors. Because each donor can save three lives, 1,539 lives have been saved or helped in our son's memory. He is still contributing to the medical field and saving and improving lives, even though he is no longer physically present.

Colin was a registered organ donor, so we decided to have a Donate Life table set up at every blood drive to promote and encourage organ donation. We have had over 100 people, mostly high school and college students, sign up to be organ donors. Another way we try to increase organ donation awareness is to offer a scholarship to high school seniors at the school he graduated from in 2014. The students can choose to write an informational essay or a personal story about organ donation and submit it to us. We read each essay and choose one scholarship winner. The winner will receive a check made out to the college that they have committed to attend. They can use this toward tuition, books, or supplies.

Colin's tissues have been transplanted into 279 recipients in the United States and several other countries. We have received two thank you letters to date. One was from a female cornea recipient who wanted to thank Colin for the gift of sight and the other was from a young man who received Colin's meniscus and was hopeful he would be able to dance at his upcoming wedding.

Colin played hockey since he was six years old. He was very thankful we allowed him to play and supported him because it is an expensive and time-consuming sport. Colin was a goalie on his high school hockey team from 2009–2014. We decided to give out a hockey scholarship to one youth hockey player each year. We asked the youth coaches to nominate a child that is at risk of not being able to play due to a family illness or financial struggle. We then pay for one year of hockey dues to allow that child to play for another year.

My husband, Mike, son Evan, and I all got memorial tattoos a few weeks after Colin died. My tattoo is on my left wrist and has angel wings with a heart in the center and a halo above. The heart has Colin's fingerprint inside and is outlined in red. I also used his handwriting from a Mother's Day card. Under the angel it says, *I love you mom, Colin*. I see it all day, every day. I love to show it off and tell people I meet about Colin. My husband gave me an urn necklace with a small amount of Colin's ashes in it, and I wear it every day. That way, he is physically with me as well as in my heart and memory.

I try hard to focus on the fact that Colin was born and lived instead of the tragedy of his death. It has proven to be very challenging but is getting easier over time. I noticed I started favoring purple items for Colin's birthstone, Amethyst. I usually include a purple heart emoji on my Facebook posts and in texts to friends and family. We planted a purple lilac and some other purple flowers—forget me nots and bleeding hearts—in our yard in his memory. Colin also had a pineapple shirt that he liked to wear so they have become a symbol of Colin for me as well. I see pineapples everywhere, have purchased a lot of pineapple items, and received pineapple gifts since he passed. We added a pineapple solar light to his garden. Colin was always the kind of guy who wore sporty clothing, but when he went away to college, he started to come out of his shell and be more adventurous with the way he dressed. He started to wear funky socks like his college roommate, Brad, and we now wear his socks and give crazy socks as holiday and birthday gifts. It's a small way to carry on the things Colin enjoyed and puts a smile on our faces and others'.

We were given a set of wind chimes in a flower arrangement for the funeral. We have had them hanging on a shepherd's hook in our back yard since that day, and the gentle sound of them year-round is peaceful, soothing, and now brings me joy.

I have always had anxiety about something bad happening to one of my boys. I used to think that I would never survive if one of them was in an accident or became ill and passed away. When my worst nightmare happened, I didn't think I would ever get through this loss. It's been a long, hard road over the past four years.

My advice to other mothers who experience the loss of a child is to give yourself all the time you need. Take things slow. Don't have high expectations of yourself and don't be hard on yourself for things you think you should be doing. When friends and family ask what they can do to help, you may not even know what to tell them. The only help you need is for them to bring your child back, and you know that's not possible. Let them cook or order you a meal and drop it off on your doorstep, so you don't feel inclined to visit if you don't feel up for it. Don't make plans or promises to people because you may not feel social when that day arrives, and you don't want to hurt anyone's feelings. I operated like this for the first couple of years and sometimes still do.

I recommend that you get some fresh air every day. Move daily by walking or stretching so your body doesn't ache. Try to remember that each person deals with their grief differently. Learning to understand this will help you manage your relationships with your partner and other children. There is no right or wrong way to grieve. Talk to and about your deceased child. Keep your child fresh in the memories of those he loved and that loved him. Be open to the signs. Your child will send them when you are ready to receive them. You don't know it yet, but you will get through this, and you will be able to hug them again one day.

Tracy Montesano, Colin's Mom

Tracy Montesano is a mother of two boys. She resides in Rochester, New York, with her husband, Mike, and 22-year-old son Evan. Tracy earned a bachelor's degree in social work from SUNY Brockport College in Brockport, New York, in 1993. She is employed part-time and works with children birth to age three and their families in the New York State Early Intervention Program. Tracy provides ongoing service coordination and case management for children in need of speech, special education, physical, and/or occupational therapy.

She lost her beautiful son, Colin, four years ago at the age of 21, from a sudden, accidental fall 25 feet from an apartment rooftop. Tracy enjoys talking about Colin and keeping his memory alive. She carries on his legacy in numerous ways. She hopes that you will get to know and love Colin from reading her chapter and that you will find some morsels of hope in her story.

Email: 0316tracy.montesano@gmail.com.

If you would like to make a donation toward either of the two scholarships she offers, please mail your check to:

Canandaigua National Bank Wealth Management

Basin Park Financial Center

1150 Pittsford-Victor Road

Pittsford, NY 14534

C/O Kirsten Johnson

585-394-4260 x36067

Webster Schroeder Organ Donation Essay scholarship: please specify on your check that your donation is to be added to the Colin Montesano *Scholarship* Fund.

Webster Youth Hockey Dues scholarship: please specify on your check that your donation is to be added to the Colin Montesano *Hockey* Fund.

Please include your address as any donation made is tax deductible, and you will receive a receipt in the mail.

MIA

Still Right Here

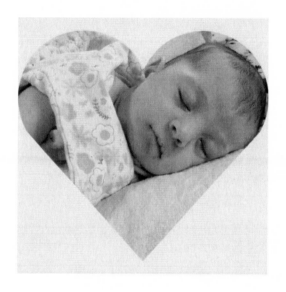

"I truly believe that my baby is still right here," as Suzanne Giesemann so wonderfully wrote in her book *Still Right Here: A True Story of Healing and Hope*.

This is our story:

We were already parents of two beautiful daughters when we found out we were expecting again. My husband and I wanted a big family, so we were thrilled to find out we were having another daughter. Everything during the pregnancy went extremely well. There were no signs that something was wrong.

Mia was born on January 5, 2020, at a healthy weight and beautiful, just like an angel. Of course, she was all pink-red, wrinkled, and covered in a thin layer of vernix, but she . . . was . . . perfect.

I didn't hear her cry once she was in the doctor's arms, so I asked my husband, "Is she breathing?" Her older sister Arianna had to be suctioned after birth to get rid of some mucus that blocked her breathing, but that problem was solved in a minute. My husband said, "Yes, she is breathing," as the delivery doctor brought Mia to my chest. Looking at the new miracle in my life lying on me, my eyes filled with tears of joy. I was never happier. My husband quickly snapped a picture of us to send to the family.

What I said so far sounds like a beautiful story with a happy ending. But what happened next was going to shatter our world.

I noticed that Mia was struggling to breathe, and she was taken from my arms after a few seconds. She was moved to another part of the room where the doctors suctioned her and tried so hard to help her breathe. They did this for about 30 minutes, but it seemed like forever to me. My arms were so ready for her, and I was so excited to feel her warm skin against mine. Foolishly assuming I would have her back soon, I tried not to worry and sent a text to my best friend with her picture. Then I read my family comments on the picture of Mia sent by my husband. Everybody was congratulating us and cheering for Mia's arrival. All this time I was keeping an eye on Mia, and I heard her attempts to cry, but thought nothing bad of it. They should be done soon, I thought.

The doctors were having difficulties removing the mucus in her throat, and Mia continued having difficulty breathing. They decided to take Mia to the neonatal intensive care unit (NICU) to keep an eye on her. Before they left the room, Mia was brought to me and I got to hold her again for just a few seconds, but those seconds were heaven to me.

They rushed Mia to the NICU and left me with empty arms. "We'll bring her back in half an hour," they said. That never happened. The room was quiet. This was not what I expected. My husband left with Mia, and I was alone in the room.

Three grueling days passed with Mia still in intensive care. She was having a very hard time breathing. She could not feed. She could not swallow properly. Something was terribly wrong. She was put on IVs, and I was able to pump and give her a bit of colostrum a few times a day in a tiny spoon.

After three days, the doctors still didn't know what was wrong with her. It was not a matter of choosing between diagnoses, they had no diagnosis. It was incredibly scary. In the meantime, Mia was struggling to survive.

We were transferred from our local hospital to SickKids Hospital, the best hospital for children in Canada. I had no doubt that once we got there, everything would be ok. We were in the care of the best doctors in the world.

Once we got there, a battery of tests began, but still no diagnosis. A week passed. Two weeks. Three weeks. Three weeks in which our daughter Mia suffered so much! She had breathing spells which meant she could not breathe for ten to thirty seconds. It was incredibly painful to watch her go through this. She was intubated on and off, and she was put on a respirator multiple times. The nurses were suctioning the mucus from her throat all the time to allow her to breathe. Her heart rate during those spells was plummeting, and she would turn blue. It was hell on earth.

She was getting my milk through a tube in her little nose. She was getting nutrients and fluids through IVs. She was having trouble resting because, even in her sleep, those hellish spells would happen, and she would wake up from sleep not being able to breathe.

I was spending the days with her and sleeping at home some nights and in the hospital others. When I was at home, I did not talk, I did not eat, and I cried constantly. When I was putting my girls to sleep, I could not talk much, and when I did, I was sobbing, telling them I miss baby Mia. Toward the end, I did not want to go home at night. I wanted to be as close to her as possible.

Part of the testing done was genetic testing. The doctors told us from the beginning that it would take approximately three weeks to find out the results. In the meantime, they were keeping her alive, but there was no progress in her condition. On the contrary, she was getting worse.

Imagine seeing your baby barely surviving, asking the doctors— the best doctors in the world—what is wrong with her, and they respond, "We don't know," for three whole weeks. They mentioned it might be something genetic, but in my mind, everything would have a cure. They told us multiple systems were affected, which is a sign of something genetic. So, I was thinking, *They can help her with swallowing by doing this surgery. They can help her with her sight by doing eye surgery and same with her hearing. They can give her all the missing minerals and vitamins for proper growth, and everything will be ok.* I knew that something was terribly wrong, but I was ready to fight.

When the diagnosis came, Mia was almost one month old. I remember my husband and I were called into a small room that was immediately filled with doctors, specialists, nurses, and a social worker. Then the geneticist revealed the diagnosis: Mia was suffering from an extremely rare genetic syndrome, so rare that it doesn't even have a name. It was called 10p Deletion Syndrome because the short arm of the 10th chromosome was almost completely missing. There are only 45 documented cases in the world, and none of these children had exactly what Mia had—or what she didn't have. Sadly, missing so much genetic information was catastrophic for her body. Her condition was incompatible with life.

Mia's condition got worse. She was having multiple spells at the same time, leaving her breathless for minutes and minutes, with just a few seconds of air in between spells. She was not able to breathe on her own. She stopped developing. She was just surviving . . . barely. At this point, they had to put her on morphine to make her suffer less. It seemed that every moment she was awake, she was struggling to breathe; and even when she was sleeping, she would still wake up desperate for air.

Words cannot express what I have seen. I have seen my little baby gasping for air so many times and struggling to breathe while desperately moving her arms and legs. It is something that no mother should go through. Every time the nurses would resuscitate her, I had to be strong and talk to her to keep her calm. Tears were falling down my face as I was trying to be strong for her. Sometimes I would turn my face for a second and hope that she would catch her breath. It was too much to take, but I am not trying to make myself important in this story, Mia is important. If I suffered watching her, I can only imagine how much she suffered going through this. I wanted to take her pain; I wanted to die so she could live, but that was not an option.

34 days—this is what she gave me on Earth—34 precious days. And then, on February 7, 2020, at 8:20 in the evening, she took one last breath and crossed the veil. She was in my arms. My world collapsed.

I will never forget the doctor saying the words officially, announcing, "I am very sorry to say that Mia has died."

My husband and I spent a few hours watching her and holding her little breathless body. It all seemed surreal for me. This cannot happen to me. I am a good person. I believe in God. Why did this have to happen? God, why are you punishing me?

I was never going to leave the hospital. How could I? But then, the nurse that was assigned to Mia that night told me gently that I could stay longer, but she had to get Mia ready, "I have to put her in a . . . bag . . . sorry . . . and take her downstairs." I knew I could not face seeing my baby put in a black body bag with a zipper. That is when I decided to leave. I was heart-broken. As I was leaving the room, the kind nurse was holding Mia in her arms and told me, "Don't worry. I'll take good care of her."

I took one last look at Mia. She looked like she was sleeping.

It was close to midnight by now and my husband and I left the hospital in silence. Broken. Devastated. Asking ourselves if this is just a dream. It didn't seem real.

The following months are just a blur. There were lots of tears, moments of despair, and moments when I did not want to live. I wanted to be with Mia as much as I wanted to be with my other two daughters who were alive. The love for my three daughters is exactly the same. Then, how could I be here on Earth when she is not? I did not speak much, and I did not communicate with my family more than necessary. I had a lot of support and love from my family and friends—a lot—but I rejected most of it in the beginning. I wanted Mia back, I did not want support and love. What I wanted they could not give me. So, I did not ask, and I did not accept anything that was not Mia.

They say time heals all wounds, but that was not happening as the months went by. The pain of not having my sweet baby was killing me . . . slowly. The guilt of me living instead of her was too much to take. How can I enjoy life when my baby is *not*? I hit rock bottom about six months after Mia left Earth.

Then, something amazing happened. First, let me tell you this: nothing would be more amazing than having Mia in my arms right now—physically—nothing. So let me rephrase, the *next* best thing happened.

I met an incredible angel mother named Claudia. She introduced me to a grief support group called Helping Parents Heal. Although I strongly wanted to believe—before I joined the group—that my baby still exists, it was healing to hear this group's open discussion about the afterlife. When I heard the stories of so many parents about the communication they have with their children, I felt, for the first time after Mia passed, that I could have joy in this life. I never intended to leave this world, but I had such a gray vision of living in pain and despair my whole life. I probably sound selfish to the mothers who never had a child pass. They probably think, *But you have your other two daughters. You have so much to live for.* But an angel mother who has other children here on Earth, would probably understand me. Yes, you can have joy in your life again, but that joy is diminished immensely because you cannot share it with all your children. So, when I heard there is a possibility I can communicate with Mia, I felt alive again.

Little did I know that Mia was already communicating with me. All the signs I received from Mia since her passing, I either dismissed as being my imagination, or I didn't know were signs from her. I want to share with you the incredible communication that I now have with Mia, and how it all started.

My friend once told me her child-in-spirit communicated to her, conveying, *you missed so many signs!* Upon hearing those words, I was going back in time trying to figure out how many signs I missed. I am sure there were many. *Please forgive me, my child. I was not ready to look for you.*

I never stopped talking to Mia after she passed—sometimes quietly in my mind, sometimes out loud in a calm voice, sometimes crying desperately. In the beginning of my journey, it always seemed like a one–way conversation, but it was not.

About a month after Mia passed, she sent me a cloud with her baby face. It is clear as day. Nine months after she passed, she sent me two clouds with her face, in the span of a morning hour. Although I was happy that I could take photos of these images, I still attributed them to my imagination. Now I reached a moment in my journey where I cherish these photos like gold, and I keep them on the wall above my desk.

I received another beautiful sign from Mia a few months after she left Earth. It was summer, and my other two daughters and I were walking through a forest. Almost every day last summer, we walked through a forest to reach one of the beautiful shores of Lake Ontario. I would let the girls walk and play on the shore, and then we would enter the same forest taking a different path and walk back toward the parking lot. Walking through the forest and going to the beach were the only two activities I was able to do for the first six months after Mia passed. Even this was too much to handle most days, but I did it for my daughters. Some days I would feel a bit of peace being in nature, almost like nature was the only thing that could—at some level—connect me with Mia. Little did I know how much nature was going to connect me with my baby.

That particular day, we took a meadow path through the forest on our way to the lakeshore. As soon as we exited the forest, my oldest daughter, Arianna, noticed a baby deer to our left, about 50 meters away from us. I have walked this path hundreds of times over the years, every single summer. I never saw a deer. That day was special. I started my video camera and the girls slowly walked toward the deer. It did not move until the girls were about two meters away from it. This beautiful creature, noticing the girls (and probably me behind them), gently lifted her head from the grass, looked at us with love, and slowly left. The deer was not startled, but was almost saying, *my message was sent.* I was amazed how a wild baby deer was not scared of three people approaching her. It took me a few months to understand Mia sent that deer to tell me she is alive and well. I am so glad I have that moment on camera, so I can enjoy it anytime I want. A precious moment.

In the same summer after Mia passed, two other amazing things happened for the first time in my life. One day in a forest, a tiny bird landed on my palm, gently and slowly picked up some seeds with her beak, seemingly unafraid (like the deer), then flew out of sight. A couple of months later, while I was on the patio of a beautiful cottage deep in the forest, a hummingbird flew right in front of me, stopped centimeters from my face, looked deep in my eyes, and flew away. How often do you get to lock eyes with a hummingbird so close that you can catch it? It was an amazing experience, and I thanked Mia for the message.

I miss my baby every day. Every second. I miss her physical body, her warm touch. I will miss her taking her first steps and the many other milestones we won't get to celebrate. There are things that I will not see in this realm, but there are things I can see, even though my baby is not here. I see that she is a loving, compassionate soul. She made sure, from the first days of her transition, to send me signs in the clouds to let me know she was ok. I see that she loves her sisters because she sends them signs too. I see that she is funny, because she turns my computer off when I need it the most. I know I can count on her to send me a message when I am feeling down. I know she knows what's best for me and helps me with that. I have no doubt the people I've met since Mia passed are the best people to help me in my journey. Mia knows I have to grow as a soul, and she is sending me amazing help. I know how Mia communicates now. I also know that she is always trying to find a new way to communicate. She is amazing. She is unpredictable. She likes to surprise me.

One day I asked Mia for a sign. I make sure I don't demand the sign, but I ask her from my heart. I like to choose signs that are not easy to find. Being winter, I asked Mia for a cherry. Do you still wonder if your loved ones are here? My younger daughter, three years old, drew a cherry on a drawing board that very night. I can assure you that Sonia never drew a cherry in her life. But this one is perfect. The photograph I took is my proof.

Another day I asked Mia for an elephant. A couple of days later, I picked up an old notebook that I hadn't opened in more than a year. On the second or third page, there was an elephant felt sticker that my younger daughter, Sonia, probably put there a long time ago. That warmed my heart.

I make sure not to ask for signs every day. Our children love us very much, but they don't want us to be dependent on signs. They want us to grow spiritually on our own. They will help, but we have to do the hard work. Imagine asking for a sign from our children every day, and they provide it. Then, one day, you don't get a sign. You panic. *Where are they? Did I do something wrong? Are they gone? I'm never going to hear from them again. Was I imagining things until now?* Our children do not want us to go through this torment. They do not provide signs on demand, but trust me when I say, Mia has never failed to give me a sign when I asked. Maybe it was a few days or a week after I asked for it, but I got it eventually. I just needed to learn to have patience and not to rely on signs from her as I continue my journey.

My daughter loves to play with electronics, especially with my computer and my phone. How do I know it's her? Because unexpected things happen only when I talk about her, or I'm involved in an activity regarding her.

The most recent sign I received from her was amazing. One morning, I was cutting strawberries in slices for my daughters, and one of the strawberries had the letter M carved inside it. Not a heart, not a circle, but the letter M. From Mia. My heart melted.

All communication with Mia is intense. I still have goosebumps thinking about the reading I had with a famous medium from England. This medium did not know who I was. She never saw me before. She told us (we were a small group) that she was feeling the presence of a baby in spirit: a girl. I froze. I felt the blood leaving my upper body, going down toward my feet. My hands became numb and cold. I barely spoke the words, "It might be my daughter." The medium then continued to say that the little girl is having problems breathing. She touched her neck with her hands and said she felt it physically. She said she is feeling a lot of phlegm in her throat, which was exactly what Mia went through.

Then I was told two things that no one else knew outside of close family. The first thing that Mia told the medium was that a cross is sitting on her chest. I was speechless. We buried Mia with a little cross on her chest. Amazing. Then Mia wanted to let me know that she is watching me. She said I read a lot. So true. Then the medium started to highlight with her hands. She said, "Do you highlight in the books? I can see you reading and highlighting." Double amazing. This is what I do: I read books, then I read them again, and I highlight the most beautiful passages because I want to remember them.

The next thing the medium mentioned was Harry Potter. Do I watch Harry Potter? Am I a fan? No, it was even better. The previous day, my friend and I were talking on the phone about the famous Arthur Findlay College in England. It is one of the most renowned schools for psychic sciences in the world. We were amused by the fact that people were comparing it to the famous Hogwarts School in the Harry Potter movies. This was what Mia was trying to tell me—that she heard our conversation. She was probably amused by it too. Then the medium said that Mia was showing her a needle in the right leg, which was again incredible because Mia had a catheter inserted in her right leg. It is called a PICC line. Then she felt her left hand was itchy, which is where Mia had a cannula inserted. The medium moved her right hand to show that she was pulling out the cannula. She said, "*I want them out.* She is pulling all the tubes and needles out." I was in awe. Mia was there. She was showing me her struggles in the hospital, not to make me sad, but to validate that it was really her.

Then the healing messages began. She said, *I'm so proud of you, mom.* She said she knows I am doing better. I felt immense joy hearing those words. She said, *Mom, I am ok. And you are going to be ok.* All my worries melted in that moment. I was so happy to hear this. Then she described butterflies and nature, and she said, *I feel better when I am in nature,* which is so true. What a wonderful message from Mia. It wasn't the only one I got through mediums, but this is the one I keep the closest to my heart.

I never knew there are so many ways you can connect with your loved ones in spirit. In fact, even now, a year into my journey, I am still learning. One of the first ways I communicated with Mia was intuitive writing. This happened about six months after Mia transitioned. My friend Claudia told me about this communication method, and I said I would try it just for its therapeutic purpose. I confessed to my friend later that I didn't really believe I would communicate with Mia. I just thought it would be a good idea to write down my emotions to release them. The day of the intuitive writing webinar, I did a short meditation together with the other mothers in the group. Then I started writing. I already had some questions written down for Mia, and now I was just writing the answers. When I started writing, I thought I would not be able to put down a single word, but the words started pouring out of me. I could not stop. The release of emotions was so intense, seeing question after question being answered in words that did not seem like my words. I would like to share with you a part of this incredible experience.

I asked Mia, *Are you ok?*

Yes Mommy. I'm a big girl now. I am not alone, Mommy. Can you hear me? It's so quiet here. There is so much light. Don't cry, Mommy. Someone is holding me.

Did I do anything wrong?

I know you think you could not protect me. You did not do anything wrong. You were not supposed to change my path. I am here with other children where the only worry is that we miss our mommies. But someone is holding me.

Are you alone?

No, no. What do you mean "alone"? I love you, Mommy. I know you are worried about me. I know. "Mommy," what a sweet word. You are going to have me again. Do you know that I am also waiting for that moment?

Who is with you?

God. Angels. Family. It's quiet. We laugh. Flowers. Water. Quiet. Someone is holding me. Your grandmother. Mommy, it's so nice and warm.

Where are you?

Somewhere you cannot understand.

That was the beginning of my writing communication with Mia. I cried so much I could not bear the emotion. It was incredibly healing, so I decided to do it again. I filled page after page for months with beautiful messages: some validating, like getting a message or phone call the next day, some just messages of love. She sent me a poem too, on the morning of January 1, 2021.

The night before, right at midnight, I was pretending to be OK in front of our guests and my husband, as they were getting ready to begin the countdown to the start of the new year. Inside, I was crying desperately, as I wanted so much to feel my baby in my arms. Right at that moment, I heard three knocks in the window. My heart froze. No, it's not possible. I am definitely going insane. Mia cannot do that. I said, "Happy New Year" to my husband and to our guests and I quietly sipped some champagne, still shaken by the knocks in the window. About an hour later, one of our guests, who is Mia's godmother, pulled me aside and whispered, "You are going to think I am crazy, but right at midnight, there were three knocks in the window." I started crying. Mia was there.

The next day I got the following messages from her, through intuitive writing.

Mommy, I have no greater joy than to see you believe. Yes, I was there last night, celebrating with you. Yes, I am real. I exist. I am.

Spread your wings and fly. It is your time to shine. Nothing can stop you. This is your path. Grow.

The more you believe, the more you can feel me. Trust your instincts. Doubt is making me fade away. I am still here. But you can't feel me if you doubt.

I am sending you peace and love. Yes, I am here. Yes, I am here.

Somewhere over the rainbow, angels fly

Should you doubt this world, you will cry

Believe with all your heart, and you will see

That I never left you and I am still me.

Love from your heart, heal from your soul,

Fulfill your destiny, fulfill your goal.

Rest in peace at night with my hand in yours,

Trust the divine, and trust in the source.

Forever you are. You and me, side by side,

The more you will see, the more you abide.

Although it may seem I am lost in the sea,

I am stronger now than I will ever be.

Your love gave me strength to stay, not apart

But close to you and your wonderful heart.

Rain, rain, go away, bring another peaceful day,

Trust in God, and you will see that I am here to stay.

Angels fly and angels sing,

Here I rest on a beautiful wing.

They bring me so I can be close to you.

If you open your heart, you'll know that it's true.

Someone who has not been through the trauma of losing a child might read this book and say, *If this mother is receiving signs from her child and she is positive that her child is well, why is she still grieving?* Have no doubt that we still miss our children here in the physical. We long for their touch, we want to say "good night" to them and we want them to say, "I love you, Mommy." We want them to play with their siblings, their cousins, and children in the park. Have no doubt we consciously live through every single missed milestone or moment we wanted to see in their life: their first step, their first words, their first date, their wedding day, their children. Grief never goes away. It's how you grieve that's important.

I encourage all grieving mothers to have their bad days, to cry until they have no energy left, to feel those feelings for their children. Those feelings arise from love. Without those feelings, we wouldn't write this book; we wouldn't read this book; we wouldn't support each other. Without our tears, we wouldn't be human. I am human. I cry and miss my precious child. I don't want to not be human. Missing her is loving her, and I want to continue to love her every second of my life.

Mia is not always with me. I do not feel her energy all the time, and there is a purpose to that. She doesn't want me to depend on her. She wants me to be strong on my own. My path is my path. She is my guide, but she will not do the work for me. She will not fulfill my purpose. I have to do it on my own. The fact that I don't feel Mia's energy at all times makes me cherish it even more when I feel her around me. I know she is never too far. But when she is close, her energy is so strong that I feel very comfortable talking to her out loud, "Oh, you are here!" My heart fills with joy. Can I scientifically explain that energy? No. Call it mother's intuition, mother's infinite love, mother's connection with her child. Mia surrounds me with her energy and we are both shining. Did you ever feel you can't stop smiling because you can feel your child there with you? It's an indescribable feeling.

I don't think of my baby as "gone." Yes, she left her physical body, but she never left my side. She comes to me when I need her the most. She lets me be on my own when I need to grow spiritually. In a way, I feel that she is an older, more experienced soul than I am.

My blessing is to know how to rise from my down days. I give my love to Mia that way, by missing her, and then I gather the strength to love her in a different way—by building her legacy. She was pure love and that is what I want to spread around me. I think about her, and I pick up a handful of love, and I spread it around. I send it with the wind.

I want to share a little bit more about the organization Helping Parents Heal. About 9 months ago, I started to have this strong feeling that all the information and the people that I encountered after Mia's passing were important in my survival. Nothing happened by coincidence. I truly believe that Mia guided me in the right direction because she wanted me to survive and thrive. All the new people I met and all the new information that I read or heard brought me one step closer to where I am today.

Yes, I can say it loudly. Today I am strong. I am broken into pieces, but I am strong. I am falling apart some days, but I get up and start over. There is immense power behind me. Power like I never had before. I am grateful to Mia for giving me this power.

My love, my sweetheart, thank you for being here for me. The biggest help came from Mia when she made me part of the Helping Parents Heal family. Yes, a family. I am still in awe, and I appreciate and admire Elizabeth, the founder of Helping Parents Heal, so much, for what she accomplished. Her organization helped me and tens of thousands of other bereaved parents. I could not have written this chapter without feeling and taking in the love and support of the Helping Parents Heal family.

Ramona Vizitiu, Mia's Mom

Ramona Vizitiu lives in Toronto, Canada. Her professional background is in the legal industry. She is the mother of three amazing daughters: Arianna, nine years old; Sonia, three years old; and Mia, one year old in Heaven.

She grew up in Romania and immigrated to Canada when she was 25 years old. She always believed in God and that there is more to life than we can understand, but her true spiritual journey began when her beautiful baby Mia passed away. She started reading, listening, and experimenting with everything connected to spirituality and life after life. That is how she got her daughter back.

Knowing that Mia is still here with her gives her the strength to carry on. She lives with Mia by her side and encourages all parents who have lost a child to open their hearts and let their departed children communicate with them. She says not to doubt that their souls are alive and always with you. She hopes Mia's story will reach all the mothers who need to hear it. If there are any Romanian-speaking mothers of angels who read this book and want to reach out, you can contact her on the Facebook group, Helping Parents Heal - Ajuta Parintii sa se Vindece, where they openly discuss experiences with loved ones in Heaven.

AARON

Our Eternal Bond

My name is Camille. I am the mother of four, three boys and a girl, and grandmother of one adorable six-year-old. My eldest boy is in heaven. Before having children, I was a critical care nurse, which was an extremely rewarding career. I also spent time as a medical technical consultant for feature films and TV, filled with exciting moments. Later, I settled into investment management, which has made for a relatively quiet transition toward retirement. But, the most fulfilling and joyous calling of my life, above all, has been motherhood.

On September 23, 2019, I received the news that no parent ever wants to hear. The police arrived at my door to tell me that my son fell to his death. He was only 31 years old. Even when given the news, I had a hard time believing it was true. It felt like I was in a bad dream. My mind couldn't take it in all at once. The shock and trauma of it was too profound.

No one expects to receive the news that their child died. It is not life's natural order. Our brains are not programmed for it. Some of us, like me, pray every day for our children's safety, health, and happiness. We assume that those prayers are heard and will be answered.

A couple of days before his accident, Aaron and I had dinner together at our favorite pizza place. We laughed and joked as usual, and we talked about his future. He was planning to buy and renovate a town house and wanted advice about the best way to finance it. He had a serious, well-thought-out plan. Three days later he was gone.

He did tell me he was tired. He said that he wasn't sleeping well and tried a sleeping pill, Lorazepam. He was going to try to get some sleep. Only, it was not Lorazepam; it was counterfeit Fentanyl. I am sure he didn't know what he took.

Fentanyl is illicitly disguised as prescription pills by criminal manufacturers and is responsible for a rising number of accidental overdose deaths. But how and where did he get it?

There is still an ongoing investigation into what happened. The circumstances are confusing, and the findings are puzzling and inconclusive. All that is known is that Aaron ingested Fentanyl and fell. I know in my heart that he never would have knowingly taken it. The moment I heard about his death is forever cemented in my brain. The flashbacks to the day the police came to my door hit with the force of a tidal wave of shock and trauma.

When I was five months pregnant with Aaron, I had an out-of-body experience. I found myself floating near the ceiling, looking down at my body lying on a bed. I felt like a coagulation of particles, or points of light. I could see everything in the room and could sense all the energy of the universe. I felt a pull, or attraction, toward the energy outside. I looked for easy escape routes from the room, like a screen or a vent, through which I knew I would meet less resistance. I knew all about the universe, and that I could travel through it and explore it as I pleased.

Just before leaving, I glanced back at my body to say goodbye. I noticed that I was pregnant and wondered if being outside of my body would somehow harm the baby in it. In a sudden rush, I was pulled back into my body as particles of light rushed away from me in the opposite direction. Just as suddenly, I came to. I dismissed the event as the result of a fever. I have since learned that it was much more.

The happiest day of my life was the day Aaron was born. He was perfect. It seemed like the sun was shining from his angelic face every time I looked at him. His eyes were bright, and his face showed the wheels inside his head were always turning. His sleep was always short, maybe so he wouldn't miss anything. He was infinitely curious and full of smiles.

When Aaron was still an infant, it became apparent he was ahead of developmental expectations. He said his first words at eight months. He could speak in sentences before he was a year-and-a-half old. At 15 months, he could identify letters of the alphabet. He played video games with my friend's six- and seven-year-old sons, and he was actually playing.

When Aaron was two years and ten months old, he loved to go for walks with me to the nearby shopping center. He made sure we took change with us to give to the buskers along the way. He liked to put the coins in their open instrument cases. He loved it if they played a tune for him.

One day, he insisted on taking some coins to school with him. He wouldn't stop crying until I told him he could take them if they stayed in his pocket. An hour after I dropped him off, the principal called. I thought that she was calling to tell me that some kid choked on one of Aaron's coins. But she said that Aaron gave one to each student telling them to put their coin in the charity box. She said that she had never seen a child that young do something like that. I was immensely proud of Aaron, and at the same time, relieved.

Aaron was a strikingly beautiful child with dreamy blue eyes, light brown hair, and a peaches-and-cream complexion. The elementary school he attended required academic testing results to be in at least the 95th percentile. Aaron tested in the 97th percentile. He did very well in school, made lots of friends, and his teachers loved him.

The Steven Spielberg movie, *Jurassic Park*, opened when Aaron was five years old. He begged me to take him to see it. The trailers looked too scary for a five-year-old, so I told him that he was too young to go, but he could already outsmart me and was adorably persuasive. I gave in and took him to a matinee.

After the movie, I wasn't sure how he had been affected by seeing it, and I was a bit afraid to ask. So, I asked him what his favorite part of the film was. He promptly responded that he liked the herd scene best. He said the graphics were amazing, and at first, he thought they were Velociraptors because of their bird-like legs, but then realized they were Gallimimus. I was, of course, speechless.

When Aaron was about 12 years old, we moved to Ohio. It was another upheaval, and to make matters worse, by the end of the same summer, we all moved back to Toronto again. He seemed to handle the frequent relocation well, but under the surface he was not OK with all the moving.

Aaron was at a tough age, 16 years old, when his father and I divorced. He was deeply affected. It was evident. He was profoundly disappointed. By the time Aaron was 18 years old, at the age of his own consent, he refused to see a counselor. He was given his own apartment, credit card, debit card, and a sports car. Aaron drifted into an unhealthy lifestyle and social group. He began to experiment with drugs.

We cut him off from what we had given him due to drug use. He came to me in desperation. He agreed to get off drugs if I let him move back in with me. After some difficult adjustments, Aaron was on the road to recovery, health, and stability. I was quite proud of him.

At the same time, I feared the slippery slope of rehab. Underneath my disguise of strength and helpful determination, I was scared for Aaron. Fentanyl had recently reared its lethal head on the streets. There were daily news reports of hundreds of Fentanyl-related overdoses and deaths. Aaron told me he would never go near it.

Illicit drug pushers make it easy to get deeper into dependency. Now, criminal manufacturers are disguising Fentanyl as other, less harmful drugs, or they are hiding it by mixing it in with other drugs. The drug-related death toll among young people today is staggering. Hence, my fears.

During the time he lived with me, Aaron became himself again. He was a pleasure to be with. His bright smile was back. He worked hard and accomplished a lot. He overcame addiction and went back to school. He completed his degree in business management and administration and worked as an investment analyst. He moved into his own apartment and continued to do well, but for years, he lamented over his broken relationship with his father. I don't think there are many people who can come as far as he did under those circumstances. It takes superhuman strength.

Aaron and I were so close. We said, "I love you" every day. We shared our triumphs and struggles. My love for him was unlimited and unconditional. I had so much pride in my son, and he deserved every ounce of it.

Around 28 to 30 years old, he was settled into himself, more mature. He found a relationship with his father that worked for him and began to let go of the one he wished they had. He was beginning to forgive his father and to express empathy for him. Just when all seemed well, his life ended.

My grief from losing my son is unfathomable. The pain in the early days was crushing and excruciating. Grief is disorienting, confusing, and paralyzing. It is at least as deep as my love for him and that will never stop. I still have days when I feel adrift and untethered; those days are exhausting. Some days I feel like I cannot live without him.

I could never have imagined or expected any of what happened. The disbelief of losing a child is not hard to understand. No one expects to outlive their own child. Losing Aaron has changed me in ways I never would have known. My heart is still broken and forever will be. I lost a part of me when he died, and the me I used to be is gone forever. Who am I now? Who will I be?

My doctor put me on sedatives when I told her I was in a state of shock after losing my son. Breathing hurt. My chest was crushing in on me. I couldn't take a deep breath. It felt like I was having a heart attack. When the police came to deliver the terrible news, I just sat there speechless. I could barely move. I just stared into space.

I barely remember sitting in the office at the funeral home. I agreed to whatever the staff there told me needed to be done. No one expects to prepare a funeral for their child. It was surreal, but my shattered heart still knew what Aaron would have wanted. Even in that state of shock, disbelief, and fog, I set out to honor him and his wishes.

I don't remember much of Aaron's funeral, but I do remember insisting that Aaron would have wanted everything traditional. My concern was for his transition to the afterlife and that his soul would get there. I'm still not sure how I got through it.

I remember feeling like I should not be at my son's funeral. It was like being in a horrible nightmare that was not going away. I just wanted my son back. Where was he, and when was he coming through the door?

After the funeral, people and food were coming and going. Most people came over to me to express their sympathies and condolences. There were a few who said surprisingly hurtful things, meaning well, but not knowing what to say. A couple of people asked me how it happened. I guess their curiosity got the better of them. I responded calmly, "It doesn't matter how it happened. It matters that it happened."

It was all so sudden. There was no sign, no premonition. Aaron's life was just beginning, and he had everything going for him: intelligence, kindness, generosity, wit, capability, and magnetism. He was making plans and going places—the world was his oyster. Aaron was moving up to bigger things. I was so proud. I was right by his side, through all of it, thick and thin. He was supposed to be here, and I was supposed to be cheering for him all the way, my whole life. How could this happen? How could he leave me? I will never know the answers because there are no answers to questions like this.

Within days of Aaron's passing, I took the charm bracelet he gave me from my jewelry box and put it on. It was all I could think of that would provide me a constant tangible connection to him. I haven't taken it off.

A couple of days later I started keeping a journal of my grief. My friend strongly suggested it. She said, "Write everything down so you don't forget." I started right away. Grief was affecting my memory, so a journal was a good idea. I found it therapeutic. I felt a continuous connection to Aaron through my writing. The distraction provided me some relief too.

Reading feels like you are with a friend who knows exactly what you're going through. Books have been my companions in grief. I read so many books on grieving and loss. They help me so much, and I like to pass recommendations forward, which makes me feel like I can help someone while I'm feeling so needy.

I took an online course in writing about my grief. It helped me through the pain, and to be a better writer at the same time. As I wrote down my feelings and experiences in my journal, I began to notice my grief lifting. I kept going back to it to feel better. About a year after his passing, I realized my journal was a record of my son's life that I should turn into a book about him for the family and future generations.

I went to a bereavement counselor that a friend recommended. It was cathartic and therapeutic for me, so I took my kids for some family sessions. They are grieving too, but their grief is different from mine. They came to me for support in the early days after losing their brother. It was hard trying to help them when I felt so helpless; but they are my children, and I want to help them. Having the support of a counselor has been one of the best decisions we all made. I still see my counselor. I still have those hard and painful days. I am sure I always will.

I started back at fitness sessions with my trainer two weeks after Aaron's funeral. I had to force myself to do this in the beginning. All I really wanted to do was stay in bed. But I already knew that physical fitness would make me feel emotionally better, so I dragged myself to my little work-out corner of my house three times a week. I took walks every day, as being outside in nature felt soothing. I have stuck with it because it works.

Over time, the shock of sudden and unexpected child loss morphs into an unwelcome acknowledgement of its reality. The sorrow runs so deep that it permeates every aspect of life. It creeps into every corner and crevice of your existence until it has taken substantial residence within your being. You become a stranger to yourself. Everything is changed.

I was Aaron's mother for nearly 32 years. Then one day, on September 22, 2019, I wasn't anymore. That is how it felt. I know I am not the person I used to be, and I never will be that person again. I guess I will have to get to know the new person I am, and that I'm becoming. I will have to recreate myself. At this late stage of my life, it won't be easy, but I am taking it one day at a time.

Aaron helped me to know who I was. He was my eldest, and being his mother was everything. I have tried to take some baby steps toward an existence without Aaron physically here. It has been really tough. We were always there for each other. I hope he knows what a support he was for me.

At some point in my journaling, it became clear to me that I could help others. I decided to turn my journal into a book. It became a labor of love. It was helping me and giving me a renewed sense of purpose and honoring my son and his life.

I titled my book *Aaron's Energy: An Unexpected Journey Through Grief and the Afterlife With My Brilliant Son (Aaron's Energy)*. I self-published my book and put it for sale on Amazon. It has been a huge learning curve and a fulfilling way to focus my love for my son. In his honor and memory, proceeds from the sales of my book are being donated to mental health and addiction care and research. My hope is that it offers comfort and support to anyone who needs it.

I even created and designed a webpage on my own, https://www.aaronsenergy.com/, with links to purchase, rate, and review my book. You can also see news, upcoming events, and a list of recommended reading and grief services.

Aaron was spiritual his whole life and I think his spirituality helped him heal quite a bit from his struggles. He devoured books on religion and history, and because of his highly analytical mind, he could offer enlightening interpretations of the stories. His verbal intelligence was remarkable, and he could make difficult concepts easy to understand.

I started a memorial fund in Aaron's memory that goes to creating a welcoming social network for young people. The program will be in Aaron's name and will be for young adults whether they are religious or not. Everyone will be welcomed and accommodated, and there will be opportunities for socializing, learning, private consultations, life skills, and mentoring. Aaron often spoke of his concern for young adults facing these issues today.

One day in October, out of the blue, I heard Aaron's voice. I was in the car on the way up to the lake house. The trees outside were beginning to change color. The highway was lined with reds, bright yellows, and oranges. I began to cry when I thought that Aaron would never see this phenomenon again. Tears were streaming down my face and, suddenly, I heard Aaron's voice say, "I see it." Then, he said again, "I do see it Mom." I gasped. His voice was loud and clear and very much his voice.

He went on to say that the way he sees colors now is unlike anything I can imagine. Colors beyond explanation. He can see the energy that the trees are emitting. It certainly made me feel that he was with me. I could tell that it was him by the sound of his voice, the character of his speech, the tone, the words, and way he spoke. Plus, the things he said surprised me. They weren't things I had ever thought of.

Of course, I still doubted that it might be me hearing my own thoughts. But Aaron told me I could hear him better as we left behind the *noise* of the city. The less noise, the less interference, and we can connect our energies more readily. By noise, he doesn't mean just sounds, he means distractions of any kind.

I think about Aaron constantly. Whenever I hear from him, I feel better. When I feel less anxious, upset, and depressed, I hear from him more. At the cottage I hear from Aaron a lot. I wonder what it is like where he is. I ask him questions, and many times, he answers. He told me things do not work the way I think they do, and no one alive can understand until they are where he is. He told me that everything operates on a flow of energy throughout the universe.

He sends me signs: birds, butterflies, dimes, and electrical and Wi-Fi disturbances. He has sent me orbs of light shooting in the dark that I was lucky to capture on film. I have seen his name in the clouds. I have found dimes, telling me he is watching over me, and hearts in unusual places. I began to understand his messages and signs better by connecting the dots.

Calendar firsts are particularly difficult for grieving people—to say they are "difficult" is a gross understatement. I still have some really tough days with my grief: anniversaries, birthdays, and holidays are extra hard. Those are the days that we think more of our loved ones. The constant thoughts trigger feelings of anguish and grief. We feel like crawling under a rock. I have learned to tell myself I must get through the trigger days by doing things I find comforting.

I try not to dwell on the circumstances surrounding Aaron's death. We may never know the whole story. I might have to accept that I will never find out exactly how Aaron's accident happened. I already sense that it won't help me feel better to know. Knowing doesn't bring Aaron back and dwelling on it makes me feel depressed. I am not able to live in the delusion that I'll wake up one day to find out this was all some kind of nightmare and life will return to normal. I tell myself that the connection with Aaron in this life is worth facing the reality.

Love is our connection. Love is energy that draws us together throughout time and through whatever form in which we exist. We must be open to love whenever and however it comes, even in our sadness. Grief is the deepest expression of the love we shared in life and continue to share in infinity.

My son will always be a part of me, just differently. I remember him with no greater joy than before the accident. We had a close bond and an enviable mother-son relationship. He was always so kind and considerate. He was generous, warm, and loving. He could reason from such an early age, and we had more intelligent and enlightening conversations than I have had with anyone else. I want to remember him for all of that. I used to say that Aaron had an *old soul*. His qualities were numerous. He was wise beyond his years, highly intelligent, intuitive, and insightful. He was witty, sensitive, and curious. He was also kind, generous, loving, and forgiving, with limitless warmth and consideration for others. He had a magnetism that radiated from him.

I have established more than one charity initiative in honor of Aaron. I read that it's a good thing to do while grieving a profound loss, and many people do it. I feel I can keep Aaron's interests and concerns alive and direct his energy to them. Aaron cared very much about many issues, and funds will be directed to support causes close to Aaron's heart. Money from the purchases of my book goes to those causes.

I was all ready to be a relaxed, retired, mother of four and grandmother of one spending time on a beach. That was back when I thought I had a choice. Now, I am a mother grieving the loss of my child and trying to be supportive of Aaron's three siblings, while I try to figure myself out. I'm taking it one day at a time. Some days, I am taking it one breath at a time. Writing is getting me there.

I put my energy into my writing, and it's taking me on a new journey. It's like an adventure. There are twists and turns, and discoveries. I have to fall on my feet and remain standing on this roller coaster of emotions, and I have found courage and confidence I forgot I had. Every day is a new chapter full of learning, especially learning how to connect with Aaron

Aaron told me the reason he is able to connect with me is because I remain open to it. He said his energy is always present and available. He said many souls cannot stay with their surviving loved ones for long, because they do not maintain the energy balance necessary. It can be because their grief is too profound, or they are too busy with life's distractions, or their minds are not open. For whatever the reason, they make themselves difficult to connect with. Aaron often reminds me how to control my complicated emotions and distractions so he can make connections with me. I practice with him often so he stays nearby.

Nature is soothing and nurturing. That is why we call it *Mother*. Whenever I spend time outdoors, I feel calm and comforted. Like Aaron says, we enter an exchange of compatible energy when we immerse ourselves in nature. We feel closer to the source of our creation. Nature takes care of us, and it is up to us to take care of nature. It helps us connect to one another and to the world.

We are living in a disconnected world. Political division is rising. Disquiet is epidemic. People are trying to come up with ways to relieve their pain, grief, depression, loneliness, and PTSD. Communities are trying, countries are trying; yet we seem to be getting further away from personal connection and deeper into suffering. This approach isn't working.

My book, *Aaron's Energy,* is about connection. It is about the exchange of compatible energy. I am hoping that Aaron's messages in my book will help make the world a better place for everyone. I think we are currently witnessing the universe balancing energy. If *Aaron's Energy* could help create understandings and clear up misunderstandings, maybe we could learn to exchange energy with ourselves, each other, and the universe. We could lighten each other's personal load of pain and grief. Maybe, through energy connection, we can turn things around.

Because it is necessary to be part of the flow and balance of universal energy for this to happen, we all need to learn how to connect with it. Visualization works well for me. Some people feel that meditation helps them find tranquility within themselves and others do deep-breathing practices. There are so many different methods to try. I have heard that some people find music soothing. There's also sound therapy machines and apps. The important thing is to find what works best for you to quiet your own mind.

Here is how I make my connection. I sit or lie down in a quiet place where noise and interference is minimal. I close my eyes and imagine a picture of what the energy around me looks like. In my mind, it looks like tiny points, or particles of light, streaming around me and through me. Some are moving faster than others, some are going through me, and through all the objects and people around me, even my dog. Animals are expert energy exchangers.

I picture in my mind some of the energy staying in me for a while, then flowing back out into the universe. Some of it is staying in the objects, the people, and the matter around me. Some energy is flowing past me, bypassing me for other destinations. In this trance-like state I can see auras everywhere. I see them around people and things. Everything and everyone emanate energy. Some people can see it.

The energy I visualize flowing into me gives me comfort. It relieves my pain and grief. It motivates me to exchange this soothing energy with others, providing them with a similar feeling, that they might, in turn, exchange with someone else. It makes me feel like I am connecting with compatible energy. It is in this state of balance that I'm able to connect with the energy of the universe and Aaron is there.

I have reinvented myself after the most devastating loss of my life. I have retained most of who I was, but it hasn't been easy. I would do anything to have my son back, but that is just not reality. Writing my book has been of immeasurable help to me. It is already helping others. Aaron tells me that we work together from both sides across the veil.

I have met so many wonderful people who I otherwise might never have met. I joined a support group for bereaved parents called Helping Parents Heal. It is a worldwide group of grieving parents helping each other. I have made friends who understand my journey, and this group has given me an opportunity to help others. I don't know where I would be in this journey without their kind and loving support. They are a significant part of my story, and of Aaron's. I imagine that our children have all met across the veil and have brought us together. Being a member of Helping Parents Heal led me to contribute to this anthology.

Aaron's Energy expanded my understanding of love and loss and of life and death. My openness to possibilities has widened beyond what I thought were the ultimate limits.

Camille Dan, Aaron's Mom

Camille Dan is the mother of Aaron and his sister and two brothers. She has professional experience as a critical care registered nurse with a BScN and BPsych and as a medical technical consultant for feature films and television.

She is currently president and founder of a private investment management firm. She is a philanthropist and hospital board director of Sinai Health System Foundation and a member of various charity groups.

She is the self-published author of *Aaron's Energy: An Unexpected Journey Through Grief and the Afterlife With My Brilliant Son.* The cover art for her book, and its second edition, have been lovingly created by Aaron's brother Jonathan Dan.

To learn more about Aaron, you can visit the following sites:

- www.aaronsenergy.com
- Aaron's Energy: Bereavement Angels and Spirit Companions (Facebook)
- @aarons_energy_book (Instagram)
- Aaron's Energy, @camgig (Twitter)

AMORA

God's Greatest Gift to Me

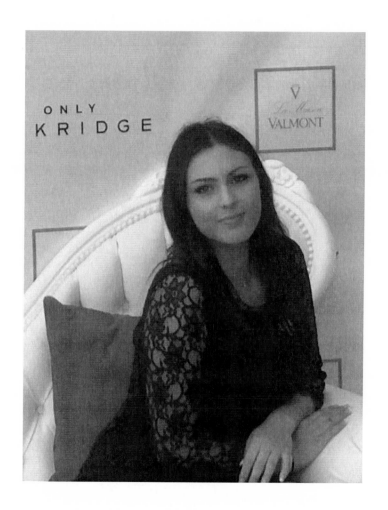

The scars I bear are many, most you cannot see, as they are hidden deep inside of me. Shame, regret, pain, suffering, and trauma—the wounds are way too deep. They sink down, as far down as the deepest darkest coldest blue sea.

You see, I am a grieving mother, this story is mine, and most would not believe it by just looking at me. I am a survivor of the worst pain imaginable: the loss of a child, so horrific; yet this story is real, raw, and painful. Every day I wake up to this nightmare, and I relive it over and over. It's mental trauma, PTSD, and you can't get it out of your head. No matter how hard you try, it's always there, like a screeching sound in your brain that makes you want to pull out your hair.

Now I know why people take their own life after a child's death; it's the burning regret and the white noise in your brain that never ends. From the moment you wake up until you go to bed, it's always there, like a burning blister or a broken limb. It feels like my heart will never heal. But I have to live my life somehow and go on because my journey is not over yet. I miss my beautiful baby girl Amora every minute of every day, and hopefully, sharing my story may help you know there is a light at the end of this long, lonely tunnel ahead called "bereavement."

Many will judge you, feel uncomfortable around you, or look at you funny. You may lose friends as many of them won't understand your pain or your journey, so keep the precious few you do have close to you and your heart.

My Beautiful Daughter Amora Parissa

Let me introduce you to my beautiful Amora Parissa, a once-in-a-lifetime daughter. This Pisces beauty was born on March 10, 1999, in Vancouver, British Columbia, Canada. She came in like a force of nature at 7 a.m., and all the power went out downtown, including St. Paul's Hospital for one full minute, which felt like a lifetime for me. I was worried about the power and the machines in my room, but I thought this was definitely a sign from God. My labor was 23 hours long. I pushed and pushed, but she was stuck under my pelvic bone. Two epidurals later, long, painful forceps pulled her out . . . and voila, there she was, my beautiful baby girl. I always said my daughter loved me so much she didn't want to leave my womb.

We named her Amora Parissa because it means "love" and "angel face," like the Eiffel Tower in Paris, France. The tower is shaped like an A and the P stands for Paris. How could I have made this beautiful gift? I just couldn't believe it! My Amora was born with beautiful blue eyes which turned to the most amazing emerald olive green. What a miracle and blessing she was.

When you lose a child, you don't truly realize the enormity of it. You made this beautiful human being inside of you for nine months. You share DNA: a baby's fetal cells cross through the placenta and enter into the mother's body. This is just one reason why mothers generally have more of a connection to their child than fathers. There is consistent longing and yearning for your child whether alive or not. At home or traveling, you will always worry about your child because of the bond you share.

Since the death of my daughter, that bond has only deepened and I came to realize that true love is not that of man and woman, it is the unconditional love of mother and child. That love is eternal and reaches beyond death. There is no greater bond, and no one can ever break it. We are each unique, and once we are gone, we will never be replaced.

Amora was the best baby. She slept through the night and hardly cried. When she would nap, I would pick her up and bring her back to the couch where she would fall asleep on my shoulder, her head resting on my chest. I can still feel her sweaty head on me to this day. I would look down at her lips, and we would fall asleep together for another hour at least. I remember even having to go to the bathroom, but not wanting to get up or even move, for fear of breaking the intensely strong bond between mother and child.

I cry every time I hear "Silent Night" and a French children's Christmas song that played in a Starbucks coffee shop one day while my daughter slept on my shoulder. They both remind me of the special bond between a mother and her children. These were special memories that will forever be sewn into my mind and heart.

I remember taking Amora for walks in her stroller on Robson Street in Downtown Vancouver. She would be so happy watching the people as we strolled along. Amora loved animals, especially bunnies. She had two cats growing up, and in her last year, she rescued her beloved dog, Ceely. She was a very kind and compassionate person and was loved by many. She was very social with a great sense of humor and always stood up for the rights of others. She made people feel special.

Amora went to Ridgeview Elementary School and graduated in 2017 from West Vancouver Secondary School. She loved to play soccer, had a great talent for art, and in her early years, played the piano. She loved Ricky Martin since she was young. She used to sing along to his videos and concerts, "Ricky Martin go go go," she used to say. We spent summers at the beach or the pool. Amora was a very good swimmer and learned to swim at an early age. She had many hopes and dreams, and like most teenage girls, she loved hanging out with her friends. She enjoyed fancy things and loved stores like Sephora and Victoria's Secret. Her dream car was a Mercedes Rover-style truck. She also loved baking with her grandma, movie and popcorn nights, music, and concerts. Watching baking shows, eating chocolate chip pancakes with coconut, and going out to dinner were some of her favorite things to do. She always got a special birthday cake from China Town—she loved to be spoiled and feel special.

We were always struggling, so Amora worked hard at several jobs to help me out. She went to school and then worked evenings at the Cactus Club in Coal Harbour, Vancouver. My proudest moment was when she helped me with my Sotheby's event a month before she died. It is called the Luxury and Supercar Weekend in Vancouver and is a very prestigious event. My colleague and I had a booth there, and we were in the VIP section. Amora dressed up so beautifully and helped us in the booth and passing out flyers around the site. I am so glad we had some time together during this last great work event. She also did some data entry for my business when she could and was starting to work more with me in the last month. She was so proud of herself, and I was even more proud to have her working for me.

Another reason I am proud of her is that she rescued a dog named Ceely from the DeKalb County Animal Shelter in Atlanta, Ga. Amora was always kind, if not a bit naïve. She had a heart of gold and would help the poorest soul on earth. Ceely had been running around the streets of Atlanta and was only 20 pounds. How that dog survived on its own is beyond me. Amora brought her home and washed her up, and Ceely is now a 39-pound healthy and happy dog. I always told her she chose the best dog in the world. She knew I was proud of her for saving Ceely and bringing her home to us. I would always make extra special things for Ceely like chicken or meat patties, and I bought her a jacket and whatever extras I could. Amora appreciated it very much.

Amora was very mature for her age and, in some ways, an old soul. She was planning to go into corporate accounting in the fall of 2017 at Capilano College. She was supposed to go on a job interview a few days after her passing at Jim Pattison Volvo in North Vancouver. She was to be a receptionist while attending school. All her dreams were tragically cut short. I found her unresponsive, face down in her bed on Thanksgiving morning, October 8, 2017, at 11:20 a.m. Her dog at her side. She was a victim of the opioid crisis in Vancouver. It was a tragic, accidental, instant death at the very young age of 18.

She graduated in June of 2017, and just a little over three months later she was gone—taken from us. She actually passed late evening October 7, 2017, and it was the saddest, darkest day of my life. I will have PTSD (post-traumatic stress disorder) forever from this tragic event.

Our Family

I was a single parent with financial pressures, so I worked a lot. I wish now I would have just stayed home, held Amora forever, and never let her go. I have a lot of regrets from working so much. I also have a son named Adello, and I was so excited to have him. I thought to myself, *I want to have someone for my daughter so when I am gone one day, they will have each other*. They were very close. They were always together growing up, playing video games, watching movies, spending time with Grandma, and traveling together on family trips. We went to places like Las Vegas (Caesars Palace was a family favorite); Hawaii (a whole month of memories I will never forget or regret); Winnipeg (to visit family); and sometimes Seattle, Wash.

Amora was the only granddaughter of four grandchildren. She was always reminded how special she was as the only granddaughter, and she often proudly reminded me and my mother of this. Amora's grandmother helped raise her because her dad wasn't around much; however, as her parents, we are both forever heartbroken. Amora and her grandmother had a special bond that can never be replaced. My mom loved Amora so much and did everything for her. Amora loved her very much too. They were close and had a bond that only a grandmother and granddaughter could understand. They had 18 blessed years of memories and special times together. My mom is having a very hard time dealing with Amora's passing. Our lives are forever changed and broken without her.

Amora leaves behind her mother, grandmother, brother, her dog Ceely, two stepsisters, and her father. She also leaves behind a loving aunty, uncle, two cousins, extended family, friends, and teachers who will love and miss her until the end of time.

I was so naive and arrogant. I thought I had my children forever and that child loss could never happen to me. I guess we are all so busy we don't let ourselves think about it, and until child loss hits your family, you can't imagine the unbearable grief. It will rip your family apart and all you knew before is gone.

Facing the Grim Reality that your Child is Never Coming Home Again

At first, when it happened, I knew for sure God must be punishing me. I would walk the seawall every morning by our home and cry while talking to God and my daughter. I would beg for their forgiveness. I would hope for rain so no one would notice the tears pouring down my face. Each step felt so heavy, like I weighed two tons. I felt like I was carrying a cross like Jesus did—that I was being punished like Jesus with thorns buried in my head. Each thought of my daughter's death was like the whipping of a leather strap ripping through my skin. I pray for her soul. I pray for myself and my family, and I pray for all grieving parents, children, and animals of course—all those suffering in this world. I would cry and curse at God. I felt like climbing to the highest mountain and just screaming, *CURSE YOU GOD, CURSE YOU LIFE, CURSE YOU WORLD*!

I had so much anxiety, I felt like I could not breathe. I felt like running for miles and miles and not stopping until I ran all the way around the world. It's like having a missing child you are always searching for, waiting to get a call from, hoping to see walk up the driveway and come home. I would imagine Amora coming through the mall doors and saying, *Mom, I am sorry. I missed you so much* as if it was all a cruel joke. But we know the painful truth.

The reality of her death is permanent. It's raw. It is the worse pain imaginable. I don't wish this on anyone. There is a constant yearning for a future that will never be: no university,

124

no wedding to plan or children to love. Gone are all our favorite things to do together like mom and daughter trips, shopping, getting coffee, taking walks, going to the beach, and just doing girl stuff. I couldn't go anywhere without sobbing like a baby for many years. She was my mini me, and when I saw her in that coffin, I was seeing myself dead too.

I still haven't gotten a headstone or written an online memorial because the pain is too real and the event itself is surreal. I just can't believe that my child is dead. I am the mom with the dead child. You see some people look at you with that uncomfortable look full of pity, and they are probably saying, *look there's the mom who lost her child.* I feel so much guilt. Why is God punishing me? Why do I have to carry this heavy cross on my shoulders and heart for the rest of my life? Why should I even want to live? After Amora passed, I wished that I would die. I didn't care if I got sick, got cancer, hit by a car, or anything. I just said to God, *Take me and bring her back.*

If I only knew Amora would be taken from me and this world after only 18 and a half years, I wouldn't have let her go for a single minute. Sometimes the pain is so bad, I feel like I would never have signed up for this if I knew the ending. Did we both know this end in our subconscious minds before she was even born? People say your life is prewritten and that our children choose who their parents are. You begin to question all the beliefs and theories you have heard before. It's like living with your heart ripped out. From the moment I wake up to the moment I go to bed, all I can think of is that my child is dead. All the *couldas*, *wouldas*, and *shouldas* run through my mind—the guilt is overwhelming—and I think of the last days, before the last weeks, before the last minutes, before the last moment . . . why did I work so much?

Signs from my Daughter from the Afterlife

My daughter is everywhere. She is in the air. I am reminded of her in the wind blowing, the streets, the sky, even our yard. She's in the music I hear and in the color of my eyes. I see her in my son, my mother, and my sister. Everywhere and everything reminds me of her and takes me back home to her.

When I talk about signs from the other side or signs from my daughter, the biggest event that makes me believe in the afterlife is the day I found my daughter's missing dog Ceely. She is a constant reminder of my daughter, and I believe she is guiding and helping us now.

I could not save my daughter, so I vowed to save her dog Ceely. A month after my daughter passed away, my ex and I were sharing access to Ceely. One day, my mother and I met my ex at the park so he could hand over the dog, but he refused to give her to me. I felt like he was punishing me by taking away the only thing that was comforting me and my mom. Ceely was our earthly connection to Amora. Unfortunately, this was typical behavior.

My ex took papers to the police station to get custody of Ceely. One month later, at the end of November 2017, he and his family took Ceely from West Vancouver, Canada, to Los Angeles, California. That's when I was forced to start a probate file and court file to try to force the return of my daughter's dog. Ceely should have been held at the SPCA (Society for the Prevention of Cruelty to Animals), until we went to court. Instead, she roamed the streets of LA in the heat and chaos for close to 10 months.

Almost two months after he moved, on my way home from Hawaii, I found out my ex was staying with his daughter in Koreatown, a neighborhood in Los Angeles. I decided to make a two-day stop to try to find my daughter's dog. The police went with me to their building, and he told me he had given Ceely away. I found this out after my court proceedings and paperwork orders were underway.

As if my broken heart could take anything else, this news made me feel like I wanted to die even more. I was sick with worry. Where was she? Who was she with? Did he really give her away? Not knowing was mental and emotional torture.

I continued to search for Ceely and on one of my many visits to LA dog shelters, a lady at one of the shelters said, "Maybe he gave her to homeless people?" My heart sunk even more. I thought, *If that's so, we'll never find her. They will never take her to the vet.* Ceely had a chip, so my only hope had been one day getting a call from a vet saying, *Are you looking for a dog named Ceely?*

Amora's dad and his family kept saying to me, "Ceely is in a good home in California." I even had a few dreams of me asking my daughter, *Where is she*? She said, *Mom, she is at Park Royal* or *Mom, she is at Aunt Mary's.* So, I went to my best friend, Google, and I searched for all these key words. I started posting my stolen dog papers in the surrounding areas and animal clinics from Downtown LA all the way to Laguna Beach. I would walk the seawall daily and I would close my eyes and say, "Ceely, if you are out there, someone loves you and is looking for you!" I would say this almost every day and I would beg my daughter to please help me find her dog. I promised her I would bring Ceely back home to our home.

Finally, we served my ex a paper saying if he didn't return Ceely, he would get a daily penalty of $100 dollars until he returned her to us. He then gave the court three photos of a homeless couple with Ceely but said he had no idea how to contact them.

It turns out it was true, and after many months of lawyers serving papers, bailiffs, dog sites, pet detectives, travels to LA, car rentals, and hotels, on September 11, 2018, we found Ceely. It was a miracle! There was no other way we could have found her in a city the size of Los Angeles, than through the power of our mother-daughter connection, Amora's guiding light, and God's hand. Ceely belonged back with us because it's what Amora wanted, and I think she knew the only way to help heal our broken hearts was through the unconditional love of her beautiful rescue dog Ceely. The grief of not being able to save my daughter overwhelmed me but saving Ceely gave me some peace.

I also want to thank the powerful network of the California Lost and Stolen Dogs sites and a woman named Jo Martin, one of three people who spotted Ceely in the last month leading up to her rescue. I am forever grateful for her and all involved.

What Helps me Get through in Life and Manage my Grief

An older male friend told me one day, in a very matter-of-fact way and to my face, "You think you are the only one?" I felt offended at first, but those words helped me very much. Once I went to the many grieving parents' sites all over social media, the newspapers, and TV, I saw the daily postings of parents that lost not only one, but two, and even three children at a time. It was only then I realized that God was NOT punishing me. Here were so many others like me, living through this mental anguish and hell every day. You just have to learn to live with it like a horrible injury that lands you in a wheelchair or paralyzes you, permanently.

Realizing I was not alone was the only thing that saved me. I would go to these sites to get inspiration on how to survive, how long the grief may last, what parents do to honor their children's memory, and how I can help other girls or youth my daughter's age. For example, I give a $500 scholarship in my daughter's honor to her high school every year called the Angel of Hope Scholarship. I plan to plant a tree in her memory this year on the British Properties Boulevard. We used to go there and take family photos when the boulevard was a sea of pink cherry blossoms. I was lucky enough to get a beautiful pink cherry blossom tree, and I plan to put a plaque there and plant flowers around the base like tulips, daffodils, and hyacinths. I look forward to hanging things from it on holidays in her honor.

Just before she passed, her favorite color was pink. Now I honor her with everything pink. She also has a stepping-stone named Un Amor with a few of her ashes underneath and a beautiful statue tribute in the middle of it. It's a tribute walkway, and a part of the Compassionate Friends Group in North Vancouver. The Compassionate Friends Group is a worldwide organization supporting grieving parents everywhere and providing a safe haven to grieve with no judgement. In the beginning, I used to go to them with my mom, and they helped, but, after a while, I felt more sadness going there. The sorrow felt heavy in the room, like a thick cloud whenever you walked in. Then COVID-19 happened. We couldn't meet, and I couldn't do Zoom either. Meeting in person is the best, but at least they are a lifeline if you are alone, in despair, or feel you have no one that understands.

I am forever grateful for their support, but I began to realize that the grieving does not get any easier. I felt the second year was the hardest. You just kind of live like you are waiting for Friday, as the saying goes. My favorite time is when I sleep. I hope to dream of my daughter, but then I wake up, and the grim reality hits me like a freight train coming through the bedroom. Then I just get up and persevere throughout the day. Sometimes it takes me awhile to get going or to get enough strength to face the day, but somehow, after almost four years, I am still here and moving forward with all the strength I have.

I realize I have my son, my mom, my family, and my daughter's dog to take care of. If I end my own life, it would be taking the easy way out. I have a lot of living to do, and I have a purpose to help others on this journey. It took me two and a half years to have enough strength to go back to work and to stop thinking about taking my own life for failing my daughter. What would my son and mom think? They too are grieving this horrific loss. What would my daughter think? I know she did not want me to take my own life. So, we must stay strong and persevere every day no matter how hard the pain is. I do not want to be a part of this sad bereavement group, but I am.

This tragedy, however, has turned me into the strong woman I am today. Once I realized our children are a gift and only loaned to us—that they can be taken from us at any moment—I became more compassionate, more loving, kinder, and stronger than ever. I used to work so much, but now, I walk more and observe every little detail. God made me slow down with this tragedy and has taught me to enjoy the things in my life and focus more on what really matters. I am more in tune with nature, birds, and sounds, and I live each day to its fullest potential. I don't have time for shallow people. I don't waste a minute of my day on nonsense or drama or things that add no value to my life.

I would like to end this by sharing a beautiful and powerful poem that I love very much.

When a child dies, a parent is still tied to that child. Souls, tied together across the universes. It doesn't matter the age when they passed. It doesn't matter how long ago it happened. It doesn't matter—none of it. Their souls are forever tied.

That's the love of a parent. That's the love that is more powerful than death. That's the heart that breaks and keeps breaking until their arms are filled again. It knows no discrimination based off of age, health, or time, it just is, and it always will be.

Their souls are forever tied, and there's nothing that can break them. That's the beauty of unconditional love.

From www.scribblesandcrumbs.com, a website chronicling grief after child loss by Lexi Behrndt

Holly Wood Tod, Amora's Mom

Holly is a 25-year local Ambleside, West Vancouver resident. She is hard-working and passionate about her family and community, an avid animal rights lover and activist, and proud to call British Columbia her home. She works with buyers and sellers of real estate in Vancouver, specializing in luxury view and waterfront homes. She has been successfully selling real estate for just over 15 years.

Being in sales and an entrepreneur and raised with a hard-working prairie work ethic (born in Winnipeg, Manitoba) has been the foundation in which she honed her negotiating skills. She found her true calling and passion in real estate.

She now enjoys time with her mom, son, and her daughter's dog Ceely. A daily routine of walking the seawall and going to the gym keeps her mentally strong and fit. She is also very passionate about music and makes sure it's part of her daily routine. Since the passing of her precious daughter, she has spent the last four years writing and making music.

Holly plans to write a book about her heroic rescue of her daughter's stolen dog, Ceely, also known as the miracle rescue dog. She even has her own Instagram page @ceelythemiraclerescuedog. She is proud to support the SPCA and the Alzheimer's Society with links to these organizations on her website. She is also a strong advocate of child and youth mental health. She now lives with a grateful and heavy heart, but she takes time to smell the flowers. She stays close to home now and appreciates everything in her life—every minute of each day. Holly believes life is precious and family is the most precious gift of all, especially children. They are our future.

EMMA

Glowing in the Dark

Photographer: Li Chen

When I grow up, I want to be like her.

When Emma was born, she was a sparkle of joy. When she left, she became a sparkle of light. Now she is the light that helps me navigate this child-loss dance and growing to know my own purpose. It seems this was part of both of our plans before we came into life. It seems now to be a plan that we both agreed upon, and although I came to understand and believe this, I am still so intrigued to see my signature on it. I wonder if my hand was trembling. Or was it straight and poised? Whatever the case, I know for sure that when I join Emma, we will talk about that.

When she was born, she was tiny. Ten little fingers, ten little toes, two perfect legs, and a big voice. She was my first born, the one who made me a mother. She was like my little real-life doll, full of energy, full of joy, easy to entertain and to care for. We instantly became best friends; our bond grew bigger and wider, until we became one. We felt each other, we knew each other, and we completed each other. We still do.

Emma was three and a half years old when we first came to Discovery Gymnastics. Little did we know how much she would discover, how much she would grow to love gymnastics between those walls—her natural habitat. Soon I realized my role as chauffeur for my tiny little star. She became a competitive gymnast just as my younger daughter, Elizabeth, was born. With a baby on my hip, our life became breakfast, school, gymnastics, homework, sleep, and *repeat*. It was our mantra. We lived by it. She breathed by it. Gymnastics became her passion. No matter how tired she was, she always strived for the best. She loved to be first, but she worked relentlessly for it. She was determined. She worked with passion, not because she was told to, but because she truly loved it.

We used to have our *girl talk* the night before each competition. I always encouraged her to *picture herself doing it*, whatever skill she was worried about. At competitions, I always felt her emotions from across the room, but I sent her back the confidence she needed, and I just knew she felt it and went with it for the gold. Our remote communication started to braid together during those competitions. I am so grateful for all those years of practice with her; I think they're why we are able to communicate now. Her favorite skill was to flip and tumble, and this was another great practice for when her life, and ours, turned suddenly upside down.

When Emma was 12 years old, after experiencing some knee pain for a while, and after being misdiagnosed for another while, we were told that Emma had an aggressive type of bone cancer, called osteosarcoma. After a few more tests, they concluded that the cancer had already spread to her lungs.

The information was too much for me to handle. I completely ignored the lungs part. I wanted to know what to do about the leg first. One step at a time, right? The orthopedic surgeon explained to Emma, and to us, they would have to remove her femur bone, including the knee. They could save her leg by inserting a metal rod, but she would have to have other surgeries along the way, as she grew, and the metal rod would need to be changed. Or, she could have rotationplasty surgery. This would remove the cancerous part of the femur and replace it with the tibia and foot. This is when my naïve question came, "What will she have instead of her tibia then?" "A prosthetic leg," he promptly answered.

The land under my feet was gone. I needed to lie down. The emotion struck me like lightning. I wanted to put her on my back, and run far away from there, but my legs wouldn't cooperate. How was it possible that my girl—my gymnast—with a beautiful, healthy body and two perfect legs, had cancer in her leg, which has already spread to her lungs? When? How did this happen? What did she do to deserve this? What did we do to deserve this?

My healthy twelve-year-old athlete had cancer, and she was about to start a journey that none of us ever imagined. As a family, we had to buckle up and prepare for take-off in the most courageous, brutal journey of our lives. Emma was the pilot, and I instantly became the copilot with no preparation, training, or exam. My husband, and Emma's younger sister Elizabeth, were the flight attendants, but the rest of the airplane filled up quickly with friends, teachers, coworkers, and people we didn't even know but were ready to ride with us. That was a gift that I will always cherish and be grateful for; it made our pain hurt less. We were assured that we are not alone. We got wings to fly and got ready to go through the many unimaginable turbulences ahead.

Emma started chemotherapy on March 31, 2016. We had two and a half months to decide on the surgery that would best meet her needs. Emma wanted to be able to do gymnastics again, to dance, to still be a kid. She could not imagine her life going forward without gymnastics. She was ready to give up her leg if this was the only way to follow her passion. So, she did. The orthopedic surgeon told Emma that if she chose to have limb salvage, this would not allow her to return to gymnastics. If she decided to have her leg amputated, having the rotationplasty surgery, then, with a prosthetic leg, a lot of hard work, and determination, she would be able to fly back to what she loved the most. She knew what she wanted; she knew what made her happiest. Gymnastics didn't save her life but prepared her mentally and physically to go through all that was thrown at her. It was the reason she could recover after every *fall* during this journey.

We had many arguments: I couldn't picture my beautiful, athletic daughter without a leg, but this was not about me. It was about her. When Emma told me I should care more about what made her happiest—not only about her having two identical legs—I had to step back and let her choose for herself. And she did. She had learned to *picture herself doing it* in many years of gymnastics, and I guess it took a trained mind and a lot of courage to see herself at the end of that dark tunnel, flipping and tumbling again, even though she had to give up her leg. Many times after the surgery she told me that she was happy with her choice.

My twelve-year-old chose how her leg would look, and I had no choice but to embrace it all because what made her happiest was most important for me. I just had the first lesson of how to land on my two feet without wobbling. I've learned through her that no matter what comes my way, I should rise up, brush off, and keep going, and the best way to succeed is to do everything with passion. I had to learn to see her amputation as luck rather than a curse.

The chemotherapy came with a lot of horrible side effects. We learned every day to adjust according to her needs. When a child has cancer, everybody in the family experiences the pain of it in its many shapes and forms. The attention was not on my younger daughter anymore, and that hurt her, and it hurt me, but there was no time for whining and crying. We all had no choice but to fight along with Emma and hope all our efforts would help toward her complete healing. In the first month, she lost a lot of weight, because of the poison that invaded her body. Her taste buds seemed to play a clumsy joke on her: food tasted like *metal* and water tasted like *rotten milk*.

It broke her heart in pieces to know she would lose her beautiful hair. I offered to shave my head too, but she didn't want me to play "weak." She wanted me to be strong. So, I had to find a super-mama cape. The one I found was very tight on me, but I had no choice but to wear it every day. There were days when I felt tired of wearing it and of being told how strong I was. I wanted to throw it away and just be *mom*, not *super-mom*. I had no choice but to wash it and put it on. Amazingly, I became more and more comfortable in it.

Driving Emma to the hospital to have her leg amputated was like driving to somewhere you never wish to arrive. How could I say, *It will all be ok,* when I didn't know? How could I say, *Don't worry,* when I was worried myself? What would her leg look like? What would her future look like missing a leg? How could I still say *one step at a time,* when I knew there would be no steps to take for months from that day? All I could say was, "picture yourself doing all the things you did before." I really meant it because I believed in her. At that time, at that moment, I left myself in the hands of the doctors and in the power of God.

Emma lost her leg and her hair, Elizabeth lost me, and my husband and I lost ourselves, but we could only afford to grieve for this momentarily. We had to stand tall for what would come next.

One thing we never lost was our hope that Emma would be cured, and our lives would return to normal. Another lesson learned was that there are things we cannot control; sometimes we just have to surrender. It was not easy for me to sit back and watch the whole horrible show unfold. I wanted to do anything I could to save Emma's leg and Emma's life, but so many things were not up to me, or to her, or to the doctors. We fought hard, right beside her. We were told that she could be healed. In fact, we met a few patients who had been through the same journey and were doing well. Emma was facing a childhood type of cancer, but she was fighting an adult fight; yet she did it with a smile on her face. She found a way to make her voice heard when she became an advocate for kids with cancer and a SickKids Ambassador (https://www.sickkidsfoundation.com/). She took any opportunity to spread the word that pediatric cancer is not rare, to tell the world that kids are our future, and it is not acceptable to treat childhood cancer with adult treatments. She spread the word that more effort must be put into finding better treatments and cures for kids' cancers.

We learned that pediatric cancer is different from other cancers. It needs more research, but sadly it is not considered *essential*, from a COVID-era perspective. She was in the best hands possible. An army of amazing nurses and doctors took care of Emma during her nine months of treatment, but they could only do so much.

It upset Emma that everybody knows about the pink ribbon, the symbol of breast cancer, but few know about the gold ribbon for pediatric cancer. She became very involved in this cause, and filmed commercials for kids with cancer, speaking publicly on many occasions, and never afraid to speak her mind. She wanted to make a change, ultimately so no child had to suffer the way she did during treatment or after.

Having her leg amputated gave Emma the chance to go back to what she loved the most, but it was a pain in the ass, figuratively and literally. It took lots of physiotherapy and acupuncture sessions, many wheelchair rides, and a walker for her to be able to stand on two feet again, but her goal was set, and when she put her mind to something, nobody could stop her.

Her body was already exhausted and weak, but her will and drive for gymnastics was strong and loud. After 21 rounds of chemotherapy, during which she had countless admissions, one amputation, two lung surgeries to remove metastases, countless pokes, scans, and many other procedures and treatments, she got the *all-clear* to *land her plane*, on the very first day of 2017. It was time for a new beginning, for her to shine brighter. She finally returned to the gym, to juggling between school, physiotherapy appointments, prosthesis adjustments, and naturopath appointments. Her skills came back one after the other.

She needed a special prosthetic leg to help her with her flips, and after a long process, she got a new sport leg. Now, she had a sport leg, an everyday leg, and a swimming leg. She laughed about this when she went to camp the next summer. Her friends would carry her swimming leg, and she would ask out loud, "Where is my leg? Who has my leg?"

Staying positive and keeping her sense of humor, saved us from falling apart. Behind the scenes was an immense amount of patience, tremendous and painful physical and emotional work to achieve her dreams and shine once more. After a year of being cancer free, in December of 2017, they found new lesions in her lungs. She was doing so well, bouncing again on the trampoline, doing handstands and splits, enjoying the first year in high school.

When the doctor told us the beast had reappeared, we couldn't even look into each other's eyes. It was too painful to face the truth. When Emma was diagnosed, among the many things we were told, was that she could live; but if she relapses there are no other options for her. Now, I was taken aside and reminded that her time with us is limited, and it is just a matter of how many months she would be with us. My mind was dismissive, because she was doing well, very well in fact. I told the doctor that we didn't want to know how long she thought she might live; she just wanted to live. Fully. Without an end date.

She had one more surgery on each lung in early 2018. The second one left her with one less lobe on her left lung, and consequently, with a shortened breath. They took her leg and now they took her wings! She reconciled the setback in the gym and began learning how to embrace the uncertainty.

She was afraid to go back to have any scan again. She called it "scansiety." We have tried many other ways to keep the beast away from her. She had countless IVs with high doses of vitamin C, many homeopathic medicines, and after three weeks spent with her at Hippocrates Health Institute in Florida, in April of 2018, she became vegan. All clean, but not all clear, as they found more lesions. She refused any more surgery and decided to live happy and free until she could no more.

She was open about her leg, about her story, and she shared it with everyone, on social media and in real life. One thing she didn't want was pity. She never updated social media with new prognoses. What brought her happiness the most was showing others how she could do gymnastics and dance with her prosthetic leg, how her hair grew again, how cancer didn't define her. Her wish was to inspire people; especially teenagers and kids who were going through the same pain as hers.

She used to say, "I am not the girl who had cancer. I am the girl who does flips and tricks with the prosthetic leg on the trampoline."

One day, a message got her attention, and her heart beat faster. She was invited to participate in Romania's Got Talent. She said "yes" without hesitation, despite my worries about her health.

She taught me to not dwell on my condition, to live in the moment and enjoy it. Although she started to have pain in her lower back, we all flew to Romania and watched her shine on that stage. She was tired often as the cancer progressed, but she took the biggest opportunity to prove to herself she could be on the stage again, and to show the world that *anything is possible if you put your mind to it.*

On that stage she said out loud that she would like to help kids with cancer. And that's what she did, in so many ways, until she left this Earth. Performing on that stage was one of the greatest things in her life. I will always cherish this memory.

Her decline was visible daily. The pain became unbearable at times. I was constantly beside her. We were scared of what would be next—of how much more physical and emotional pain she would endure. Most of all, we were scared of how we would handle witnessing her death.

She told me she didn't want to live anymore because life didn't make any sense to her if she was confined to her bed, not able to go anywhere, never mind gymnastics. I listened to her speaking to me as she was saying how hard she tried, how hopeful she was, and how unfair all this was. It is hard to understand how some kids make it and some don't.

"I did everything they asked me to. I did everything you asked me to. I became vegan and tried wheatgrass juice and all-natural therapies. You prayed every single night and touched me with all the holy oils. You took me to the icon of the *Holy Virgin Mary,* when it was brought in our church, to still look my own death in the face."

She said many things I didn't have words for, but deep inside I knew that was not her fault and not my fault either. She also said, "I never lost any battle, because I never picked a fight with cancer in the first place, and I didn't have the proper tools to fight with."

She was right. Pediatric cancer is way underfunded, and osteosarcoma is left way, way behind. Even though I know that, I also know deep inside there must be a better reason for this to happen. I refuse to believe that this happened for no better reason.

Emma said, "I wanted to inspire so many people and now I can't anymore." I reassured her that her videos are now all uploaded to YouTube, Instagram, Facebook, and Vimeo and people will still be inspired. You can watch Emma's performance at https://vimeo.com/419080618.

To give the pain a break, and to distract us from some heavy talks, we used to watch gymnastics until we fell asleep. We watched every Olympic Games and every World Championship from beginning to end many times. This was what we did every night.

As I was watching her and caring for her pain, I started to read *Proof of Heaven: A Neurosurgeon's Journey into the Afterlife* by Dr. Eben Alexander. I knew she would not be gone. I knew she would not be lost. I also knew she would be whole again. She would have two perfect legs, and in my pain, I could picture her being healthy and whole again. What I couldn't picture was the dying part.

One day she told me, "Mom, even if I will not be here for you to see me, I will be here in spirit. I will send you signs, and you will know that is me."

All I could answer was, "Make sure it will not be a spider or something creepy. That will make my heart jump." I wasn't ready to hear her talk about death as much as she was.

She assured me, in the same serious tone, that she would know how to *not* make my heart jump. How much I love her for knowing this, for promising this, and for keeping to her promise! "I would like to have a gold balloons release," she said one day. I knew what she meant, but I wasn't ready to have a conversation about funerals. It was already enough to watch her in pain and realize I couldn't do anything to save her. All I could do was to push that button on the morphine IV for her.

Waiting for her to get better was an unrealistic wish. Waiting for a miracle was still wishful thinking. Waiting for her to die was like accepting that I could not save her, that we all failed: the parents, the doctors, the treatments, the system.

For her, there seemed no point in living anymore; for me, it was as if I was nine months pregnant and waiting for labor. I knew there was no way out but to go through horrible pain, at the end of which I would know, even though I could not see, that my beautiful girl was whole again, happy, and healthy.

That day came. Emma had wanted to hug and kiss a real lamb for some time, and a special friend—whose daughter fought leukemia and for whom our family built a backyard playground through Emma's favorite charity, Million Dollar Smiles—brought the lamb in for Emma to kiss, pet, and feed. She was so happy! Her last wish was finally granted! I was holding her hand on the left side and daddy was holding her right hand.

About two hours after the lamb left her room, in the most peaceful and content voice, she looked up in the corner of the room and said, "Oh, my God, Mommy, it's time for me to go!"

I knew what she meant but I still tried, "Where?" as if I wanted her to tell me what she saw.

She didn't answer me. Instead, she turned toward daddy and with her last resources of power she opened her arms wide and gave him the biggest hug ever, saying, "Oh, Daddy, I love you so much." He loved her back. Immensely!

I whispered in her ear, "Soon, you will have two perfect legs, and you will be happy and free to do gymnastics again. I promise that I will always watch the Olympics with you," and this is how she finally let go of me, her dad, all the nurses in the room, and of a world she came into to change for the better.

She graduated from the university of life, and she flew back home. I knew that very moment she was not gone, and she was not lost. She just went backstage. I was ready to watch the show that she'll prepare for us from beyond the veil.

I had never watched someone die. I couldn't fathom watching my daughter dying, but here I was. Even with all the pain, it was beautiful to witness that there is something more to eternity that we don't see. She left us with a gift in that very moment. It was 11:15 p.m., April 7, 2019, when her soul made the biggest flip into eternity. I couldn't even cry. All I could feel was relief and all I could think of was that she didn't need that body anymore. It didn't serve her to be who she truly IS. She IS much bigger than that. Now she is free to do cartwheels and flips on the clouds or on top of the rainbows. She didn't deserve to die, but she does deserve to be free!

If I still wanted her to stay, in those circumstances, it would only be my ego. Even though she lived a short life, she lived with passion and had a mission that she gracefully accomplished. Who am I to keep her from letting herself go and grow more in spirit, on the path that she has? I am just a vessel who brought her into this world, and I could not be more grateful that she chose me as her mom and us as her family. Caring for her during the last three and a half years was more of a gift than a challenge.

Emma started to find hearts about half a year before she passed away: a paddle in a heart shape, a stain on her shirt, wet footprints on the pavement, and even a blood stain on her gauze after blood work. I used to tell her these are signs from God, as I know deeply in my heart that despite what we went through, God loves her.

"How can you tell me that God loves me, when He lets me suffer so much and lets other kids die? These are signs from other kids who are waiting for me there." she said.

I had no words for that.

"I am going to be next," she told me one day.

"What am I going to do without you, Emma?" I asked her.

"I am sure you will figure this out." she said.

How can I disappoint her now? She left me no room for that. She raised the bar high for me and my only choice is to live the way she did and do what she cannot do anymore. We still build playgrounds for children with life threatening illnesses through Million Dollar Smiles, the charity that was so near and dear to Emma's heart. It was no surprise to find hearts dented in a piece of wood, fresh from the package, that her friends and I were using to help build a playground in her memory. When we were done building it, as the plaque with her name was screwed on top of the playground, the song on the radio was *Stairway to Heaven*. I felt like climbing up those stairs to give her a hug for that.

Three days after Emma's funeral, Elizabeth asked me to stop at the supermarket to get something for her. I didn't feel like it. I was tired, and it was raining. I wanted to go in and out fast, so I parked my car in the accessible spot, as I still had Emma's sign.

She never liked me parking there because she said, "I am not disabled. I am just differently able."

I kind of felt guilty for doing it, but I talked to her out loud "Please, Emma, I will be quick. Just this time. Let me use your sign." When we stepped out of the car, a heart lay at our feet (a smudged piece of paper).

One step, another heart. "Oh, Emma, thank you! One heart would have been enough to understand that you let us use your sign." One more step, the third heart.

Elizabeth noticed and said right away, "There are three hearts because she tells us that she is in the car with us, and we can use her sign safely."

Right. I didn't know what I was more grateful for: the fact that Emma is with us, or that her sister put it into words for me.

Two different people came to me on different occasions, shortly after Emma flipped into eternity and told me how they went to a medium and Emma showed up. They were told that there is a girl, about 15 years old, who had her leg amputated, but now she is doing gymnastics with two perfect legs, just the way I assured her it would be. I had no doubt it was my Emma, and I felt grateful that she found a way to confirm what I already knew.

Three months after her leaving, she was supposed to celebrate her sweet 16 birthday. How bittersweet! I decided to celebrate her as if she were here. I got her favorite cake and invited her friends, and we all went to her resting place to release some gold balloons, as per her request, and a thought I always had in the back of my mind. I got twenty gold balloons just in case some of them popped. I was not surprised to see, when I arrived at the cemetery, that four balloons had burst. I was left with sixteen balloons, exactly how many we needed.

On her 17th birthday, we got to release butterflies at her resting place. One of the butterflies didn't let go of Elizabeth's hands. She decided to bring it home. It didn't move from her fingers all the way home, even while driving. We put it in our memory garden at home. At 11 p.m., he still was there. I guess he wanted to guard our home. I thought perhaps he couldn't fly, but he was gone in the morning.

In September of 2019, a few months after Emma passed away, Elizabeth and I were gifted two tickets to see Cirque du Soleil, a unique circus-like acrobatics show, that we never watched live, though it was one of Emma's wishes. As we were seated, we were amazed to realize that the spots right beside us were taken by the family who brought Emma the lamb that last night in the hospital. The seat beside Elizabeth was empty the whole time. I guess it was taken by Emma. This was her way to *set up a date* for us and finally enjoy the live show.

I didn't think of how I would survive all *the firsts* because I knew that Emma would be with me *forever and always* as she often said. I just had to sit back this time and enjoy the show that she arranged for us from backstage. I talk to her often, out loud, while I clean, cook, and drive. She comes with us every time we leave the house. I even make space for her on my right, where she used to sit on our countless trips to the hospital. I like to say that I travel in style, with my angel on my side. I ask her questions and I get the answers. There is no day I drive, and I don't see a car with the plate number *047*, which is the day when she became free, and sometimes more than once in a single drive.

One day, I dared to ask her out loud, "Emma, is this you?" The next song on the radio was "It's You" by Ali Gatie.

One day my husband yelled, "There is gymnastics on TV now!"

Oh, yes, how did I forget this? It was the World Championships. We both sat to watch.

"Let's record it," I said. We realized that the record button was already on.

My first birthday without her came with a lot of harsh memories from my last birthday spent with her in physical pain. *Is this how my birthday will look every year from now on?* I said to myself. I instantly decided to change my birthday. I always wanted to be at the beach on my birthday, but it never happened, so I decided that from now on, my birthday will be in the summer. I learned how to make it work to be happy.

On the first New Year's Eve without her, we were invited to a small party, and I instantly said "yes." I knew she wanted us to go, and she would come with us. When we got to the venue, at the entrance, we were told our table was number seven. No surprise. Seven was already a big number for us. We got to our table where two other families were already seated. When we introduced ourselves, the only girl at the table said, "My name is Emma."

My husband gets nudges from Emma too. He was thinking deeply of some beautiful memories with Emma while driving one day, feeling more happy than sad. He glanced at the radio and noticed it flickering. He remembered other times when our light flickered while we were talking about Emma. He thought for a moment and pressed the power button to see if it stopped. Instead, he started hearing the song "Spirits" by The Strumbellas. He told me that he truly felt she was there with him, on the right seat. I could not agree more.

When we raise our vibrations by staying in love rather than despair, we can meet our loved ones halfway, as they try hard to lower their vibrations from their place of love. She left me a legacy. I take any opportunity to help kids with cancer and their families. Giving back is one of the ways I keep her memory alive.

Last Christmas, we collected gift cards for the families of children on the oncology floor at the hospital. After we delivered them to the hospital, on our way back, two cars were in front of me in separate lanes, easy to spot their plate numbers at the same time. One was Emma's birthday, and one was her final day on Earth. She just told me how proud she was.

I thank her all the time, and the more I acknowledge and thank her, the more often it happens. I have my sad days too. I still tear up, but tears are good. I allow myself to be sad, but then I go forward, because I know I have a mission and a purpose, just as she did. Did I find mine yet? I am not sure, but I ask myself now, *Why am I here?* I trust she will guide me. What makes me happy now is to help other families who are where we were and assure them that they are not alone.

I am also writing Emma's whole journey and how our connection became stronger after she left, in a book called *Emma's LEGacy.* I promised her I would write. It is not easy to relive those memories while writing, but once I began, I realized how healing it is. The only way to heal is by going through the pain again, reliving it, releasing it, making peace with it, and making love with it. Sharing Emma's story with the world was one of the wishes she left on paper for me. I found it in her diary a few months after she left on the same page where her last words were—*Tell your loved ones how much you love them, because you never know when you will last see them. Give hugs, spread love, give compliments.*

Claudia Neagu, Emma's Mom

Claudia Neagu was born in Brasov, Romania, on November 16, 1976. Education and discipline were prominently valued during that time, and coupled with her love for children, she was led to pursue a profession as an elementary school teacher.

When she was 25 years old, she emigrated to Toronto, Canada, with her husband, and they still live there. Claudia has great love for her country and town and has returned almost every year since. She is a mother of two wonderful daughters: Emma Maria, her gymnast, forever 15 years old and Elizabeth Tiffany, her dancer, 11 years old. Due to events related to her daughter's illness, she had to temporarily pause pursuing her degree in early childhood education (ECE). She has now resumed and is close to completing her ECE certification.

After all she has been through, she has made it her mission to help other mothers and families who are going through the same ordeal and to find light and hope in a darkness that never seems to quell. Claudia's religion and values are of high importance to her; however, when Emma passed, she started to question her religious journey. She set out on a soul-searching mission in spirituality to help her answer the questions regarding her purpose in life. She is one of the Caring Listeners and Affiliate Leaders for Helping Parents Heal, a nonprofit organization that she likes to call the "Net F(l)ix for broken hearts." She is available for anyone who needs a hand to make this healing road smoother.

AUSTIN

Just Look at the Moon

Austin was born on New Year's Day, 1996. I loved him before he was born, but when I saw him for the first time, I knew he had my heart forever. He was such a beautiful baby with the brightest blue eyes. I started a new job when I was pregnant with him, so I could only take off for two weeks. It was so hard to leave him, but I was lucky to find a babysitter who was loving to him. He stayed with her until he started preschool.

Austin was a happy child. He was so smart and eager to learn. Even as he got older, if he paid attention in class, he wouldn't have to study for exams. He had a great sense of humor and loved to make people laugh, this continued throughout his life. He was always teasing or joking around, especially with his friends. He was active and loved when we would go to the park, and I would act just like a kid too, chasing him and going down slides. We were always together, except for when I was at work. We were pretty inseparable, even when I needed a minute, he wouldn't give me one. He was definitely a momma's boy when he was little.

Austin always loved sports. When he was very young, he started playing soccer, and he loved it, but he couldn't wait to play football. As soon as he was old enough, we signed him up, and he was so excited. He loved it so much but still wanted to play everything else. If you can think of a sport, he probably played it. He played all throughout grade school and high school and lettered in football and track. When he went to college, he found rugby and loved that too. Austin was aggressive and very protective by nature, so these sports fit him well. Plus, he loved the comradery he had with his teammates; they were like another family to him.

I always told Austin he could be anything he wanted to be if he tried hard enough. Austin had no limits. He would figure out a way to do everything. He seemed to have this aura about him. He would go on a job interview, and at times I didn't think he was qualified, but he would come home and say, "Of course I got the job!" He was social and comfortable talking to anyone. He had so much confidence. I always knew he would go far in life, or at least I know he would have.

Austin is my only biological child, but we have a large, blended family. His father has two older children, Mike and Michelle. They were really young when we started dating and I became close to them, but things just didn't work out between us. We split up when Austin was only 11 months old. Austin's father didn't spend much time with any of the kids after I left, but Mike and Michelle's mother and I became friends, so I was able to stay in touch with them, and Austin got to grow up knowing his brother and sister.

A few years later, I started dating my husband Larry and in 2004 we got married. Larry has two sons to a previous marriage, Matt and AJ. So, I was blessed with two more boys and Austin was blessed with two more older brothers. All of Austin's siblings are married with children, and he is the uncle of four nieces and two nephews.

Even before we were married, Larry became Austin's dad. He was always there for him. He took him hunting and fishing and taught him so much. While Austin was growing up, we were all together most of the time, other than when we were at work and school. Matt and AJ would come over on the weekends and when Matt turned 18, he moved in with us. Then when AJ turned 18, he moved in too. So, at one time, we had a houseful. There were some bumps in the road, but for the most part, we all got along and enjoyed spending time with each other.

The day after Austin's high school graduation he was sworn into the Army, and a few months later he left for boot camp. I know he was scared, but he didn't really show it. The day he left, I tried to hold it together, but I was a wreck. I was never away from him that long and I wasn't even allowed to talk to him for about six weeks. I told him to just look at the moon and know that we would be looking at the same one. We wrote all the time, but he didn't receive my first letters until weeks later and when I finally was able to talk to him, I knew he didn't want to be there. He was homesick, but he made it though and became a military policeman.

He seemed to find God during this time. We never really went to church, but he was going every Sunday while he was there. I really think faith helped him make it through with a positive attitude. We went to his graduation at Fort Leonard Wood, Mo. We were so excited to see him and so proud of him. I know he was proud of himself too. Shortly after, he got his first tattoo—Matthew 6:9–13—which is "The Lord's Prayer." I asked him why this verse, and he said because every funeral we ever went to this was the prayer they said, and it reminded him of those people who have passed. Wow, I definitely didn't expect to hear that, but oh my heart!

Once we got back home, Austin started college at Indiana University of Pennsylvania. Austin got passing grades, but at first, I thought he only wanted to go to school to play rugby and have fun. Austin was at that age where he didn't tell me much. He was living in an apartment close to college, playing rugby, and serving in the Army reserves. He came home some weekends and holidays. We talked on the phone a few times a week, but I didn't see him as often as I used to, so I was always so happy when he came home. I even bribed him with a free tank of gas and a bunch of food if he came home for the weekend. After a few semesters, I noticed he was starting to change. He seemed to realize that college is important, and he has to do well if he wants to make something of himself. I would call him, and he would say he was at the library. I actually asked him if there was a bar up there called "The Library." He would laugh and say, "No mom, I am actually at the library." He was growing up, he was maturing, and we were talking more again.

Holidays are always a special time for us. We would spend time together with the whole family and our last Christmas together was no different. That year, Austin was talking about going to a Steelers game for his birthday. I was a little concerned about this since the game was on New Year's Eve. We talked about it. Austin said, "Don't worry mom, don't you know I'm invincible," as he threw his arms up in the air. But Austin never made it to his birthday that year. He was in an accident three days before his 22nd birthday.

Our last night was just like any other night. We made dinner, ate together, and watched TV later. Austin decided he was going to the mall for a new belt. I told him it was cold outside, so he better get a coat. He said, "Yeah, you're right," which surprised me. He went back to his room and got the new jacket I got him for Christmas. Before he left, he was standing at the fridge with the door wide open, texting. Larry told him to shut the door. When he was leaving, I said to be careful, and I think I said "I love you," but I'm not positive. I told him this all the time, but I just can't remember if I said it that night.

I couldn't sleep that night, so I got up to go to the couch, but before I went out, I pushed on Austin's bedroom door. I thought it was closed, so I figured he was home. I fell asleep on the couch and woke up to this very loud banging on the front door. It scared me, so I yelled for Larry, and he came out and opened the door to two police officers. They asked if they could come in and if we would sit down. Then they said what no mother should have to hear, "I'm sorry, but your son was in an accident, and he is deceased." Life as I knew it ended in that moment. My heart was forever broken. I didn't believe it. I was in shock. I was in shock for probably a few months, if not a year after that.

Larry took care of everything. I didn't have the energy, because I was just so broken. Everyone wanted to come over, but I told my husband to tell them I wanted to be left alone. I even told him to tell our two other boys not to come. I seriously regret this. Our family should have been together that day and all the days following. I know they were hurting too, but I couldn't see past my own pain. I have since apologized for not being there for them. I truly hope they can forgive me and understand that I was in a very dark place.

I didn't eat anything for days. Why should I be able to eat if Austin can't eat? Why should I be able to do anything if Austin can't do it? So many of these questions ran through my head constantly. My husband tried so hard to get me to eat the littlest thing, but I didn't want anything but my son back. I couldn't understand how my heart could still be beating without him.

In the days following, I knew I had to get up and make arrangements. There was a beautiful new funeral home up the street from our house, and even though I was dreading making these arrangements, I couldn't wait to get there to see my son. When we got there and talked to the director, there were so many decisions to be made. I didn't want to make any of them, but we got through it. Then they took us into the casket room, and I picked a beautiful silver casket but the thought of him lying in there made me sick. After all of this, I asked if I could see my son. The director kind of chuckled and said, "No, you can't see him with his legs like that." I still don't know the extent of the damage to his body, but what he said still haunts me. I was so upset. How dare this man laugh. What the hell was wrong with him? We didn't say anything about it, because I really didn't have the energy to be mad, plus we still had to go to the cemetery and pick a final resting place for Austin. We knew exactly where to go. My husband and I always met for lunch and walked around the cemetery close to where we work.

A couple days later, on Austin's birthday, we told everyone they could come over. The house was full of family and Austin's friends, and I was still so distraught, but I loved hearing the stories his friends were telling us about him. I wanted to know everything. They told me so much that they even said a few times, "He would kill us if he knew we were telling you this." One of his friends told me that a few days before he left his physical body behind, he wrote on his social media page that he wants *Mansion in the Sky* by Mike Stud played at his funeral. What are the chances of this, and why would he say that? We had this song blasting (just how Austin would have played it) at the funeral home that last night before we left.

As crazy as it may sound, I couldn't wait for the day of the viewing. I wanted to see my baby so bad. The funeral home called the day before and said we could come in that evening to see him. When we got there, the doors to the room were closed. The director came and opened them. It was a very large room and when we walked in, I was hoping he wouldn't be there, that they made a mistake, but I could see his silhouette. I knew it was him. I fell to the floor and bawled. I really just wanted to die so I could be with him. At that moment, there wasn't anything I wanted more. I wasn't suicidal, I just wanted to be with my child. The fear of death was gone, and to this day it hasn't returned.

Most of the next day is a blur. So many people came through. I didn't realize how many friends Austin had, and some of the stories they told me brought to light how my son truly was. They shared things with me that I never knew about Austin, sides of him that he never showed us. A couple of his fellow soldiers drove for hours from other states to pay their respects and told us how they wouldn't have finished boot camp if it wasn't for Austin's support. Other people who had disabilities told me how Austin befriended them and always took the time to talk to them. So many stories made me proud of him. As a child, Austin was so sweet and always felt he needed to take extra care of kids with special needs or medical issues. I didn't realize it carried on to adulthood. Austin never mentioned anything about it. He didn't need recognition. He was doing it because he wanted to.

The day of the funeral was very difficult; I decided to write Austin's eulogy. So, I got up in front of everyone in the church and spoke about my son. I really don't know where I found the strength to get through it, but I did. My thoughts were that I will not be able to say anything at his wedding or when he has babies, so I have to do this for him. Larry and one of Austin's friends also got up and said a few words. It was so cold that day, but we went to the cemetery and had a small service outside. Austin was buried with full military honors. One of the hardest moments was when the service members folded the flag and handed it to me. I guess that's when I realized it was over, and I wouldn't get to see my son again.

As the days went on, I learned the details of the accident. Austin went to the mall and then stopped at his friend's house. This is the place where all of his friends would hang out when they were younger, and a lot of his friends were there that night. Then they all went their separate ways, and Austin met up with another friend. They were on their way to a party at Slippery Rock College. Austin always drove fast. I told him to slow down and wear his seatbelt constantly, but he was almost 22 years old. He thought nothing could ever happen to him.

I have been struggling to put the entire accident into words. I don't want anyone to think badly about Austin; however, when I asked him what he thought, I immediately got a reply, *Mom, I am not embarrassed about how I died. It was an accident. I didn't mean for it to happen, but it did.* So, from what I have been told, this is what happened. Austin was speeding and wasn't wearing his seatbelt that night, moments before the accident he posted a photo on Snapchat of his speedometer. He was going 100 mph and when he looked up, there was a car coming in the other direction. He swerved and lost control of the car. It went airborne.

The car clipped a telephone pool and knocked off the tops of a bunch of trees. It went a really long way. Austin was ejected from the car and died on impact. Thankfully, his friend put his seatbelt on right before the accident and walked away with a few minor injuries, but I'm sure he will have nightmares about it forever. About a week later, we went to see the accident site. Pieces of the car and Austin's college papers were scattered everywhere. I started searching the area, for something—anything—but I wouldn't find what I was looking for; Austin wasn't there, just remnants of his life were left.

Austin's friends were there the day after the accident, gathered most of his belongings and dropped them off at our house. Then, we went to see the car and clean out anything we could. The jacket I told him to grab before he left was sitting in the back seat along with the belt he went to the mall for. The rosary beads he had hanging on his mirror were still there and are now hanging in my car. His keys were still in the ignition. The cabin of the car was intact and the hardest thing to swallow is that I think he would have survived if he was wearing his seatbelt. I was so sad for a long time, but then I just got mad—mad at Austin. Why didn't he listen to me? I would actually scream at him at times, but then as a mother always does, I forgave him. He made a mistake, he was young and reckless, but in his almost 22-year-old mind, he had everything under control. Austin loved his friends and family, and he would never intentionally hurt anyone he cared about. How many times have we all done stupid things when we were young, and most of us just got lucky?

The months following, we worked on creating a beautiful stone for Austin. We bought two extra plots so we can be laid to rest next to him someday. Larry came up with the design: there is a small stone on the left with our names on the front and on the back is the Bible verse, 2 Corinthians 4:18, *So we fix our eyes not on what is seen, but on what is unseen, since what is seen is temporary, but what is unseen is eternal. (NIV)* There is a larger stone with a cross connected to it on the right with a church in the background and Austin is leaning against a tree in front. The back has the Bible verse Psalm 144:1–2, *Blessed be the Lord, my rock, who trains my hands for war and my fingers for battle; he is my steadfast love and my fortress, my stronghold and my deliverer, my shield and he in whom I take refuge.* (ESV) Then there is a bench that connects the two stones. The seat of the bench has another picture of Austin at the bottom of a staircase going up to the sky with a moon in the background, and it says, *Just look at the moon, baby, and know we will be looking at the same one.* We went back and forth with the designer for almost a year before it was perfect.

Austin was such a huge part of my life for so long. He was my whole world. I can't believe it's been over three years, and even though he isn't physically here, he is still such a huge part of my life. He is still with me. I still talk to him, and sometimes I hear him answer me. I have received so many signs and messages from him, and following are a few examples.

The very first sign we received was a couple nights after the accident. We were watching TV, and Larry noticed that the refrigerator door was open slightly, which was odd because it always slammed shut. We got up and closed it and tried many times to get it to stay open by itself, but it wouldn't. Every time it would just slam shut. I remembered how the last night we were with Austin, he was standing at the fridge with the door wide open looking at his phone.

Shortly after Austin passed, I was sitting on the floor, and I had this indescribable feeling that I needed to go to the Holy Land. I talked to Larry about it, and we booked a guided tour through the Holy Land and Rome. It was truly an amazing experience. We visited so many places that you hear about in the Bible, and we got to pray at so many churches and monumental places—places where Jesus once stood. We even got baptized in the Jordan River.

We kept thinking or waiting for something awe-inspiring to happen, but nothing really happened at the places you might think. When our tours were done one day, we went to downtown Jerusalem, and were sitting outside at a café in the town square. There were hundreds of people around and we noticed a man coming toward us. He was dirty and unkempt, and we thought he might be homeless. He stopped at our table and asked us if we were Christians and when we told him yes, he said we should have more babies because there needs to be more Christians in the world. Then he asked us if we had any children. We explained how we had three boys together, but we just lost Austin six months before. He told us he was very sorry and said he lost his daughter to terrorism several years ago and went on to tell us he just lost his wife three months prior. Then he grabbed our hands and said a prayer for us. When he was finished, he looked up at me, and he had this unexplainable twinkle in his eye, then he just walked away. We looked all around to see where he went but he was gone. With tears in our eyes, we looked at each other, and at the same time, we said we were just visited by an angel.

I don't know why this man walked to our table when there were hundreds of other people around, but I believe he was sent to us by God, and we have since been told that you don't just go to the Holy Land, you are called there.

One of the greatest gifts Austin gave me is when I asked him, "What was the very first thing you saw when you opened your eyes after the accident?" I always thought he would say something beautiful like waterfalls or streets of gold and for about a year and a half, I didn't get an answer. Then one day, when I was sitting in the woods, I asked again, and I got the most amazing one-word answer. Somehow, that one word told me so much; it was *Life*. What I understood that to mean is he saw life the way it should be lived: pure, free, and happy—without limits or fears, without any bad feelings about anything, just complete love and joy! The way he will live for eternity. This meant so much to me and still does.

I wanted to meditate and try to connect with Austin, so I read a lot about it, and I tried, but I was having such a hard time. Finally, it worked. The first few times I was somewhere else, and I wasn't able to connect with Austin, until one special day. Here is what I wrote after the meditation.

I'm outside walking up a hill where I see a big glass ranch style building. I pushed the glass door open, and I went inside. There is modern furniture like short square couches and chairs. It was bright and welcoming. I sat down on the couch. I started feeling anxious. I felt like I was in a doctor's office waiting room, but nobody was there, and my chest was hurting. I looked behind me and I saw someone walking toward me. It was Austin. He was so handsome. He was wearing a green polo shirt and jeans. He came closer and I stood up and grabbed him and held him so tight. We weren't speaking, but we were still communicating. I could feel his stubble against my face. I could smell his cologne. I said, *I love you*. I forgot everything I wanted to ask him. He told me he loves me too and he knows I am sad, but I have to believe we will be together again. He told me that he is so happy and loves it there. A tear ran down my left cheek. I don't ever want to let him go, but I sensed it was time. I watched him walk back the way he came. He turned around halfway and gave me that big happy grin of his. I walked back out the glass door and opened my eyes and I am back in this world. This connection was so meaningful and has really helped me with my grief.

I believe the best time to connect is when I am between sleeping and awake. Sometimes I wake up in the middle of the night and feel like Austin wants to talk, so I get out my pen and paper and start writing. We have communicated this way so much. Here is a communication from June 2020.

It's beautiful here. Mom, the love continues. It's amazing Mom. I'm not sure how to explain it. It's flashes of color: pinks, blues, and purples, like fireworks. It's so different. I work Mom, but I'm happy doing it. Keep trying Mom, we can connect! Quit calling me "sweet boy"! Yes, Mom, I know how much you miss me, but it's different here. I know we will be together again, and you think you know but you're unsure. Just love, Momma. Just live. It's ok. I am happy, and I want the best for you. It used to be your job, now it's mine. I love you, Momma, you are my best person. I'm sorry I didn't tell you, or show it, but Mom, you were my everything, still are. I'm not joking. I really mean it. Get to sleep Mom, talk soon. Love, Me.

Sometimes I end up with a poem. I usually forget what I write, and when I wake up in the morning and read it, it really surprises me. Here is what I just wrote in February 2021.

To the depths of my soul

lies an ocean of endless pain.

Pain unraveling with each wave of grief.

Grief so deep that it stabs like a knife

in the darkness of my despair.

168

Swimming in a sea of sorrow,

I want to breathe but the weight

is like being underwater,

You can see the light at the surface,

but you just can't get to it.

You fight the force but your heartache

Just keeps pushing you down deeper.

I know this sounds dark and desperate, but sometimes the grief is still so intense. Most days I am doing better though.

I never thought I would say that it gets easier, but it does. Don't get me wrong, I miss Austin every single day. I think about him all the time, but with the grace of God, it has gotten easier. At the beginning, I didn't want to do anything, but I knew I had to go back to work. I took off two weeks then I went back, but it was way too soon. I was so anxious, customer problems meant nothing to me. I was seeing a counselor, and Larry and I went to grief classes together, but it didn't help much. My husband never left my side except for when I was at work. He was so worried about me. I believe that God sent Larry to me. I really don't know if I could have made it without him. He is my love, my soulmate.

After about four months, I decided I needed to take some time off. I just couldn't function at work anymore. I was having nightmares, and I would wake up screaming, and panic attacks were happening constantly.

The months following, we started traveling. We found that just getting away has helped us the most.

Before the accident, we would go to Marietta, Ohio, quite often. After, we started going even more. It's just an old small town on the river with a lot of history and things to do. When we drive into town, we both feel like a huge weight has been lifted. I am happy and at peace when I am there. So, just last year we decided to buy a second home there. I know our families think we are crazy, but through all of this, I have learned that life can change in a minute. I don't want to waste any time. I'm going to take chances and try to be as happy as I can.

Late in 2019, I started going to Helping Parents Heal meetings held by the local HPH support group. It helped me to connect with other parents who understood and who were going through the same thing. It was nice to be in a place where I was allowed to talk about my son without people feeling uncomfortable. I even planned to go to the 2020 HPH annual conference but due to COVID, it was cancelled, and we started having remote meetings. It just was not the same for me, but the in-person meetings are starting back up, and I am looking forward to attending them again.

We have done many things to honor Austin since he has passed over. We purchased new uniforms for the rugby team at his college, and they had three memorial rugby games for him. We have offered scholarships, and we ran in the Pittsburgh Marathon. We will always try to find new ways to honor him.

Austin would try anything, and my goal is to continue to try new things to honor him. He was supposed to be deployed to Guantanamo Bay, Cuba, with his Reserve unit, and we talked about him getting certified in scuba diving. He wasn't able to, so Larry and I did it for him. The following year, we did eight open water dives. It is so beautiful and healing under the water. I want to honor my son by taking chances and experiencing things that I know he would love to do.

Time has made the blow a little softer. I will never be over him going to Heaven. I don't understand why, but I figure that I am not meant to understand, and someday I will learn the secrets of life and death. Until something as tragic as losing a child happened to me, I always said that everything happens for a reason. As the years pass, I am beginning to believe this again. There absolutely has to be a reason why my heart, my world, had to be shattered. Someday I know I will get the answers I crave, and the love I carry with me will keep me going until we can be together again.

I know I have changed, but I have learned to enjoy life again. I love spending time with my husband, and I am so happy for the joy I find in my grandchildren. I am truly blessed to have them, and my stepsons and their wives in my life. I am so grateful for my friends and family who have been there for me since that awful day. All these people have made my life worth living again. I intend to continue to live and thrive and do what makes me happy until I meet my son again across the veil.

If you lost a child, just remember that nothing will hurt you more than this. You have made it, even if it is only day by day. You will never get over it, but by the grace of God you will get through it with your child always by your side.

Tammy Osche, Austin's Mom

Tammy Osche is the proud mother of Austin, who tragically passed away in a car accident. She is currently spending her life with her loving and devoted husband in a small Pennsylvania town. She has been blessed with a very supportive family, who have seen how one moment in time can change everything. She is *Amma* to her two granddaughters and grandson. They help to ensure that even though her heart is broken, she can feel love again. They bring so much light and hope to what was once a dark place. Tammy's world stopped the day her only child passed away. She didn't think that she could survive without her beautiful son, but her connection with Austin from across the veil and her faith in eternal life keep her moving forward.

If you would like to connect with Tammy, you can reach her at Austinlookatthemoon@gmail.com.

RYAN

Love Has No Boundaries

We all have hopes, dreams, aspirations, and goals. As life goes on, those change with our experiences, and our reality changes as well. When I was young, I thought life could be planned, and I had control of my destiny. Looking back, I realize life is much different than I thought. All the events that happen in life (good and bad) happen for a reason. We may not always understand the reason, but we have grown to realize there are no coincidences. Sometimes we must learn to live our lives differently.

I never thought I would marry and have children. I was living in Pittsburgh, but my profession required internships that were in California. Shortly after arriving, I met John, and 35 years later, we are still together. We are blessed with three kind, empathetic, unselfish children and truly cherish spending time with them. Alex was born in 1992 and our lives changed for the better. Then, a few years later, I was pregnant with Ryan. I started to fear having a second child wondering how I could possibly love another child as much as Alex. When Ryan was born, all my fears subsided. There is no doubt you can have multiple loves in your life. John and I developed a new routine, and life was better than ever. Alex now had an incredibly special friend in his brother.

Three years later, life became more complicated but amazing. We were outnumbered by children when our third son Sean was born. At this point, we realized there was not an instruction manual for parents. Despite sharing DNA and the same parenting style, they are all unique. Alex had a quiet, laid back personality. Ryan was full of energy and more inquisitive. Sean adored his older brothers and learned everything quickly so he could keep up with them. Our fears and reservations were quickly alleviated. We could not love anyone more than our three beautiful sons. I also started to realize I was meant to be the mom of sons—this was not a coincidence. We were the perfect family of five. We all grew together learning to parent, learning life lessons, and enjoying life.

In three more years, instead of expanding our family again, we realized we had outgrown our home. We loved our first dream house and had many great experiences and memories. We were torn as to what our next move should be. After investigating other areas, we chose to move to Pittsburgh. We decided it would be the best of both worlds, close to family and friends and cost-effective housing. We could also return to California to visit family, friends, and the ocean. John and I were both blessed to be born into supportive, loving families.

We found a house in a quiet neighborhood with a large back yard. Alex, Ryan, and Sean had their cousins nearby and met new friends. It did not take them long to adjust to their new schools and get involved in extracurricular activities. They were happy and thriving. We continued to be a close family exploring different places, coaching their teams, traveling with their sporting events, and going on special vacations. We had family dinners every night. On Sundays, we had dinners with extended family at their grandparents' house with their aunts, uncles, and cousins. They had fun kickball and whiffle ball games in the backyard and even created their own games. I found a job I liked, and John found a location nearby to open his woodworking business.

All three boys had great groups of friends through school and sports. Ryan, in particular, always seemed to have a large group of friends. He had a few really close friends as he got older but always friended many different people. In school, Ryan was always praised by his teachers as being kind to everyone and listening well. He was always sensitive to other people's feelings. We did not recognize the significance of this until hearing stories later.

Ryan did not get into much trouble, but there was one time in high school when Ryan and his friends were going to a football game. They met at a friend's house to share a bottle of bubble gum flavored vodka. The driver did not drink, but on the way to the game she had a fender bender, and the police came to file a report. Ryan's friends ran fearing they may get into trouble, but his friend who was driving was frightened and crying. Ryan said he could not leave her alone. Although the alcohol in their system was below the legal limit for an adult, as a minor you are not permitted to have any alcohol in your system. Ryan and one of his friends were charged with underage drinking. Ryan called us crying and was so upset, but when we arrived, the policeman pulled us aside. He said, "He is a good kid. He cared more about his friend than getting in trouble." Ryan broke the rules, so he paid the price, but it was hard to become angry with him. He did the right thing by staying with his friend.

At this point, Alex graduated high school and went to college at Indiana University of Pennsylvania to pursue a business degree. He worked for John on breaks from school. Ryan graduated and decided to pursue teaching, so he enrolled in a program at Duquesne University. This was a perfect choice as Ryan was always amazing with children. He also worked with John in the woodworking business and had a job at a daycare. Sean was still in high school, continued to play sports, and worked part-time. Life was moving in the right direction for everyone. We continued to have meals together as much as possible, take interesting vacations, and enjoy our extended families. Although life was changing for all of us, we were still growing as a family.

Looking back, things with Ryan started to change in February 2016. Up until that point, he had a few different girlfriends who were sweet and a pleasure to be around. Then Ryan started seeing a new girl. Lauren was not very friendly. We had concerns but felt like we needed to give her the benefit of the doubt. After a few months, she disappeared. We thought they broke up, but Ryan said she was away. He later confided in us that she had a problem with addiction, and he realized she was using again. Ryan shared his concerns with her parents, and she went back to rehab. She did not contact Ryan at all for three months, but then showed up at our house at the beginning of August. She said she needed someone to go to a Narcotics Anonymous meeting with her. Ryan appeared to be happy to see her and agreed to go to support her. Ryan thought she was turning her life around. She appeared to be sober and had enrolled in a cosmetology program. Ryan started spending time with her the next two weeks and even brought her to a family event in memory of his grandfather. Ryan was excited to introduce her to his extended family. We were not sure about her, but Ryan was 21 years old. Prior to this relationship, he was a good judge of character when it came to girlfriends.

A few days later, on Sunday, I had to work and called to see who would be home for dinner. I wanted to know if anyone had ideas for what to eat. Alex was living on his own and Sean was working, so it was Ryan, John, and me. They decided they wanted Chinese food, so I picked it up on my way home. We talked during dinner, and Ryan said Lauren was at a family wedding. Ryan was in a good mood and seemed happy. We asked him if Sean could use his car sometimes for school for the time being, until we bought another car Sean could use. Ryan was so proud of his beautiful new car. It was the first car of his own. He agreed that Sean could use it the next day, and he would have Sean drop him off or ride into work with John.

I left for work that morning before Ryan and Sean woke up. Ryan got up and changed into his work clothes. When John was ready to leave, Ryan said he would be in later because he had a headache. John was frustrated but thought Ryan would come in later when Sean returned from his morning classes. Sean came home from college after his first day of class, and Ryan was home when he got there. Shortly after, Sean realized someone must have picked Ryan up because he was gone, but his car was still there. We found out later that Lauren picked him up. It was the last time any of us saw him.

I tried to call him on my way home from work to see how he was feeling and if he would be home for dinner. He did not answer my calls or texts. This was unlike Ryan. He always let us know what his plans were. Our house rule was to let us know whether you would be home for dinner or to sleep. We stressed no drinking and driving and were OK with staying at a friend's house, but all the boys knew we worried if we did not know they were safe. We left multiple messages with no response and started to call some of his friends. Sean was out and even stopped at Lauren's parent's house to see if he was there. Later that night, I received a text from Ryan's phone. The message was strange and did not sound like a message he would send to me. It read, *I'm over my boy Jack's My phone's gonna die I'm good*. I asked if he was feeling better and the response was, *Ya I'm gonna need my car tomorrow*. I slept on the sofa waiting to hear from him or for him to show up. The whole thing just did not seem right. It did not sound like him.

The next day I was off, so I had Sean take my car to school. When he got home, we started making more phone calls to friends and I drove to Lauren's parents' house. I had never met them before, but they did share what they knew about that night. Lauren had been arrested the night before around midnight for drug possession and breaking into cars. They were waiting to bail her out from jail. I feared Ryan was with her, but they said he was not, and she was arrested with her ex-boyfriend. Lauren's mom took my phone number and said she would question Lauren when she picked her up and call me. Ryan's friend Robbie and I drove around for hours looking for Jack's house, where he said he was in his text. We finally found it and spoke to Jack. He and his girlfriend said they had not seen Ryan for at least a week. He really appeared concerned about Ryan's disappearance. We reported Ryan missing to the police.

While looking for information in Ryan's room, we noticed he left his apple watch behind. He must have been in a hurry because he loved his watch. It helped us to piece information together as to who Ryan left with that morning and why.

Monday morning, Lauren started texting Ryan saying she was *in a bad way, and she needed something to keep her from feeling sick.* She said she went out and binged and now felt terrible. Ryan's messages back to her pled with her to not use anything, but she kept begging. Ryan ended up giving in and said he would see what he could get her. Per the other messages, he planned on going with her to pick up some Percocet and then heading to work. We could not see any additional messages as his phone was too far from the watch.

We also got information from the bank as to ATM withdrawals. This information gave the police a few leads.

Family and friends searched frantically for days until late Thursday evening when Allegheny County detectives showed up at our home. There is absolutely nothing that could ever prepare you for news like this. We had not slept in days, and as a parent, this is the worst conversation you could ever have. You always fear that something could happen to your child, like an accident, but not this. We knew Ryan would never torture us by not calling, but we checked all the hospitals and every other place we could imagine. Where was he? I do not even remember what the detectives said. How do you tell parents that they will never see their beloved child again? Fear moved quickly to hysteria and then emptiness. We had a house full of friends and family but no one and nothing can comfort you. It was truly *a living hell.*

The rest of the story was pieced together from the detectives' report, phone records, ATM cameras/transactions, and Lauren's original testimony (prior to being further implicated). Lauren picked Ryan up from home and drove him to get Percocet. Lauren was supposed to take Ryan back home, but then told him her ex-boyfriend was threatening her and her family. She said she had to go and meet him as she owed him money. Ryan did not want her to go alone. He felt he could protect her. They met Lott, but he had a gun and started threatening Ryan. She said he forced her to drive, and he had the gun on Ryan the whole time. He even proceeded to hit him in the head with it. They drove 20 miles away to a rural branch of PNC bank, and Lott was behind Ryan while he withdrew money. He didn't have much money in the account at the ATM, so they even went into the bank together to see if there was more in the account. Lott became angry that there was not more money. They drove to a wooded area and Lott forced Ryan out of the car. They fought, but then Lauren reported that she heard a gunshot and only Lott returned. They left him and drove home like nothing ever happened.

That night, Lott and Lauren roamed around the neighborhood near her parents' home and a neighbor reported them for breaking into cars. They were planning to throw the evidence in a pond near there. The police arrested them with drugs, drug paraphernalia, and a bag containing a gun, a phone, and keys. The police did not know the gun was used in a crime or that the keys and phone were Ryan's. They were charged with drug possession and carrying a gun without a permit. We found out they also sent the messages that evening from Ryan's phone to make it sound like he was with someone other than Lauren. Lauren chose Jack because we did not know him. They sent the message about the car so they could come and get it from the driveway.

In another few months, we found out what we knew all along. The story given by Lauren had many pieces missing. We also knew Ryan would have never been there if it were not for Lauren. Also, the only reason Lauren cooperated with the detectives was to try to get immunity. The detectives really did not believe her story completely, but said that to find Ryan's body, you sometimes must make a deal with the devil. That was very frustrating initially, because we felt in our hearts that she was responsible. Fortunately, Lauren lied under oath, and Lott provided evidence that Lauren purchased the bullets for the gun which belonged to Lauren's father. This was the gun used that dreaded day. Also, Lauren had to have unlocked Ryan's phone and knew what messages to send to us. Overall,

Ryan would not have been there if it were not for Lauren luring him that day.

Nearly three years later and multiple hearings, postponements, and changes in lawyers, Lott was offered a plea deal. It was less than the first-degree homicide he deserved, but included homicide, kidnapping, and robbery as well as multiple other robberies the weekend before murdering Ryan. Lauren was still given the plea for conspiracy to commit homicide and was given the maximum sentence possible. It doesn't bring Ryan back, but we are thankful these two criminals are no longer in society. There is never true justice when you lose your beautiful child, but we are thankful for all the hard work of the detectives, deputy DA, and the judge. They are truly unsung heroes and work every day to try to restore justice.

The days following the horrible news of Ryan's murder, we were inundated with an amazing amount of support. Family, friends, Ryan's friends, and people in the community started doing everything they could think of to let us know they cared. People showed up with tables, chairs, food, and drinks. Others cleaned the house, cut the grass, and did laundry. My sisters arranged the funeral and helped coordinate everything. There were so many details designed to make the days special and all about Ryan. Everyone surrounded us and each other with love. We were in shock, disbelief, and immense pain, but so thankful for the outpouring of support. The special planning added to the service and all the beautiful stories shared have helped us through the years. We never tire of hearing stories about Ryan. You find out so many stories you never knew.

We all knew Ryan had a very competitive side, and he was not always a modest winner. This would drive his brothers and friends crazy at the time, but this was always short lived and resulted in being the best of friends again. Ryan was a big huggable teddy bear with a heart of gold. Ryan always had time for his family and friends. He had a hard time driving by the man selling flowers on the bridge, so he frequently stopped to buy flowers for me, his grandmother, aunts, or girlfriend. He loved to buy special gifts for his family and friends. Ryan enjoyed playing basketball, baseball, video games, ping pong, and wrestling. It was a regular occasion to come home from work to a street lined with cars and a fierce two-on-two basketball tournament going on.

Several friends shared stories of exceedingly difficult times that Ryan helped them through. He listened, gave advice, and kept everything in confidence. Ryan's outside demeanor was full of smiles and a quick wit, but he also had a very wise and mature soul. A classmate from high school shared a story of how Ryan was always kind to her while most people shunned her. She moved to Montour in high school and had a difficult time making friends. She was emotional sharing that at graduation Ryan was the only classmate who acknowledged her. A student from Duquesne shared a story about how she was tearful in the campus cafeteria one day. Ryan had never met her before, but listened to how difficult thigs were for her, offered to help, and gave her money. There were many unsolicited acts of kindness and compassion shared that we didn't know about. He was even more special than we thought.

About a week later, my sisters arranged for us to meet with Latasha Batch from the Best of the Batch Foundation. This is an amazing foundation, which was initially founded after a tragedy. It has grown to be a valuable community resource for youth in the Pittsburgh area. The people there took the time to talk to us and give us some ideas of how to get started with a project in Ryan's memory. They gave us the name of a neighboring area that needed support and programming to help build up their community and were there to answer questions and get us started.

Many wonderful people donated money when they heard about Ryan, so we decided to take that money and start a nonprofit organization called Rebound4Ryan. Our family and friends came together to brainstorm what we could do to make a difference in the community. All the ideas, artwork, writing, web design, time, legal services, and money for the nonprofit were labors of love.

The ideas flowed, and the organization grew from the ground up. The purpose of Rebound4Ryan is to preserve the legacy of Ryan by combining his love of basketball with his passion for working with children. Through this program we will work together to create a positive impact in Ryan's name as we rebound from a negative and tragic circumstance.

In basketball, to "rebound" means to gain possession of the ball after a missed shot. We want to teach the youth of the community that when they miss a shot, both in life and on the court, they can rebound and move forward. In addition to basketball, the program involves mentoring to help the students learn the importance of love, respect, and community. The name Rebound4Ryan contains Ryan's favorite number and the logo, designed by his friend, has a crown and colors similar to his favorite basketball player Kobe Bryant. All the ideas, programming, and fundraisers have been supported by amazing volunteers.

Over the last four years, we have adopted a school district to donate money for programs, had a basketball/mentoring/lunch program for students, and offered scholarships each year to a student at our adopted school district Sto-Rox, as well as Ryan's alma mater, Montour. We know Ryan is right there with us through the program, and it has provided us a unique opportunity to give back to the community.

Another leg of our journey has involved individual therapy and support groups. John and I worked with several different therapists. We found you sometimes have to through different therapists to find a good match. We also found our life now is even more of a roller coaster than normal life. There may be days you can breathe, live, or even laugh. Other days, you just want to cry all day and don't even want to get out of bed. Some days you can barely think or complete your normal daily tasks. There are *triggers* that occur much more frequently. You will find that over time, you need to work on yourself, your family, and your marriage. The individuals who listened to us, gave advice, and provided resources were invaluable. Our friends are important to us, and the support groups gave us some wonderful new friends. Sometimes you need to talk with people who are in a similar situation and have similar experiences and feelings. We have helped each other through the dark days, listened, and picked each other up when we were down.

We met Elly and Yan Sheykhet as we were both presenting scholarships in memory of our children, Ryan and Alina, at Montour High School where they were both students. Ryan was a few years older than Alina, but when he was killed in 2016, Elly said it really affected her. When discussing the sad

186

event with her mom, Alina even posed the question, "What if that were to happen to me?" A year later Alina was the victim of a heinous crime. We have no doubt they are hanging out together and guided us to come together for support. Elly and Yan introduced us to a different support group just for parents, Helping Parents Heal. The group has been a great support and provided us with tools to continue a relationship with Ryan. Helping Parents Heal provides an opportunity to share with other people who understand how you are feeling and validate the communication you receive from your children. The books we have been reading, the signs and messages we have been receiving, all started to confirm our beliefs. Although the group meetings are infrequent, the support, resources, and common beliefs have been a springboard for helping us with our journey.

I have attended Reiki courses and experienced Reiki with a practitioner, which has been positive. My first experience was with an amazing occupational therapist, Rebecca Austill-Clausen, who taught a Reiki course. I read Rebecca's book, *Change Maker,* about her experiences communicating with her brother after his death. I wanted more than anything to increase communication with Ryan. Rebecca took time with me and shared her experience. She encouraged me and taught me Reiki. I have had the pleasure of attending multiple workshops to enhance communication and change my views on life and the afterlife.

We have had very enlightening and comforting meetings with mediums. I know many people are skeptical of mediums and feel they give you generic information, watching your reaction. The readings we had were not like that. All the readings were different but amazing. They shared information they could not have googled or found on Facebook. The readings were emotional and somewhat overwhelming, yet comforting. Luckily, all of them allowed us to record the sessions so we can listen again. As you listen to the recording again, you can find more information. Sometimes it helps make sense of information you were not able to process the first time.

I believe some people truly have a gift as a medium, but to a certain degree, I think we can all learn to develop our communication skills. I have been trying to slow down and pay attention to the subtle signs. We are so busy throughout the day and overwhelmed by stimuli, we often miss the communication from our loved ones. John and I have been trying to take walks in nature and spend more quiet time. This past year, along with Alex and Sean, we attended Lilydale, a community in New York that practices the faith of Spiritualism. This was an amazing setting to meditate, walk in nature, meet with mediums, attend workshops, or just relax. I cannot wait to return to Lilydale and experience more of this spiritual area and increase our communication skills.

Our relationship with Ryan continues to evolve. Ryan shows us signs in many ways. John receives more olfactory signs than I do, although we all recognize Ryan's scents. Ryan worked with John and Alex in the woodworking business. John and Alex frequently sense Ryan's presence overlooking their work. Knowing him, he is critiquing it and giving his approval or telling them that he could have done it better. Sean has communicated with Ryan mostly through dreams. The most profound occurred the morning Kobe Bryant died last year. Sean woke up and recalled a strange dream. In the dream, he was in a helicopter and excited, looking at the hillsides around him. He had never been in a helicopter before. He woke up and saw the news that Kobe Bryant was killed in a helicopter that morning. The view they showed of the crash area looked like the view from his dream. Kobe Bryant was Ryan's favorite basketball player. He painted his room purple and gold and idolized him. Sean is convinced the dream was a message from his brother telling him about Kobe's accident and no doubt telling Sean he is playing basketball with Kobe.

I only remember one of my dreams that involved Ryan. It was November 2017, and in the dream, Alex and Sean walked in the door with Ryan. They reported he had been imprisoned somewhere and had escaped. They were bringing him home, and we were all so happy to see that beautiful smile and have our beautiful son home. I woke up, and unfortunately, it was not real, and I did not know what the dream meant. Several days later, we found out that Lauren, who was still out on bail, had failed a drug test and was sent to jail. We believe Ryan was telling us this news.

We have had many experiences which we now realize were not coincidences. Cotton Candy, AKA C.C., was our dog. She became part of our family in June of 2014, when we traveled to Kentucky to pick her up. Alex and Sean did not want to go, so John, Ryan, and I took a road trip. We had a great day and Ryan was able to pick up C.C. and name her. She was our family dog, but C.C. was really attached to Ryan. He spoiled her rotten. After Ryan left his physical body, C.C. became withdrawn, until one day in September, she became terribly ill. The vet did everything possible for her, but she could not be saved. We were heartbroken to lose our beautiful puppy, but we believe she was meant to be with Ryan. The house was even more quiet now, so John started to look for another puppy. There were no similar dogs available. Suddenly, while searching one day, he found the only American Eskimo, and her name was Cotton Girl—similar to C.C. We were all going to be off for the preliminary hearing and decided we would travel together to get her. We pondered the name on the way there and decided on Cobe, after Ryan's favorite player. All our dogs had names starting with a "C," so Cobe would fit right in. When we arrived, Cobe was jumping up high in the air just like a basketball player! Was it a coincidence that we found her? We do not believe it was.

We receive many signs from Ryan, especially with his favorite numbers, which were four and his favorite player's number, 24. The number shows up frequently for us, as well as the rest of his family and friends. One of his good friends was playing baseball in college, and he said one day there was a jersey with the number 24 in the locker room. It did not belong to anyone and was just lying there. He knew it was a sign from Ryan who was one of his biggest cheerleaders. He had it framed for us and now I see it every morning.

Frequently, butterflies or birds hang around us when we are outdoors—way more than normal. The day of Ryan's funeral, a butterfly kept flying around the church catching everyone's attention. It was not just for a fleeting moment, he kept flying around as though he was saying, *look what I can do.*

When Ryan was young, he used to like to pose upside down while I was taking pictures. He would drive me crazy while I was trying to take a picture for a Christmas card or some other purpose. There was a picture of the three boys, with Ryan upside down, that was one of John's favorite pictures. He still has it on a mouse pad. It became one of Ryan's trademarks. Multiple times now, we find pictures randomly turned upside down. We know it is Ryan!

John was driving down the street one day feeling especially sad and asked Ryan for a sign. The next thing he knew, he saw a purple basketball in a yellow bucket at the side of the road. Ryan's songs will appear on the radio frequently, or we will see an array of purple and yellow wildflowers when we are driving. Several months ago, I was having a tough day and looked down to find a single leaf sitting there shaped like a heart. Another day, I was making potatoes for dinner, reached into the bag, and pulled out a potato shaped like a heart. John, Alex, Sean and I were in the car driving to a mass for Ryan's birthday when a call from Ryan showed up on the hands-free screen. We know Ryan was undoubtedly letting us know he was in the car too. The signs are too numerous to name but many of our family and friends have also received signs.

It has been a long and arduous journey for the last four years. We continue to miss our previous life with our sweet son with his beautiful smile, huge hugs, quick wit, and everything of his physical presence. We would do anything to turn the clock back. John, Alex, Ryan, Sean, and I support each other and are working to keep our minds open for continued communication. We talk about Ryan all the time, and he is an integral part of our family.

Move through your grief at your own pace and keep your mind and heart open to new learning. This club, which we are now members of, is woven with underlying pain, but we have found some amazing new friends. Our children have brought us together to support each other and work on ways to continue our relationship with our children. This unique relationship is not one that anyone would choose, but it is our reality. Lastly, don't forget there are no coincidences. Keep your minds open to the communication from your beautiful children. They are continuing this journey with us. We will never be the same, but we will move forward.

Shari Keenan Ramirez, Ryan's Mom

Shari Keenan Ramirez was born in Pittsburgh, Pa., to very loving, hardworking parents and two sisters who are also friends. She graduated from Allegheny College in Meadville, Pa., with a bachelor's in biology/psychology, as well as an occupational therapy degree from the University of Pittsburgh. Internships led Shari to Los Angeles, where she met her husband John and was blessed with three amazing sons: Alex, Ryan, and Sean. Life has revolved around growing and learning with her beautiful family and close relationship with extended family and friends.

Shari enjoys traveling, reading, and cooking for family. She has worked in multiple settings as an occupational therapist including Northridge Rehabilitation Center, UCLA Medical Center, and UPMC Home Healthcare. She has worked for 34 years with pediatric and adult patients. In August 2016, Shari and her family's lives were turned upside down when Ryan was brutally murdered. Ryan was 21 years old, full of life, and wanted to be a middle school teacher.

Along with family and friends, Shari and John started a nonprofit organization in Ryan's memory called Rebound4Ryan. The goal of the organization is to work together to provide a positive impact on the youth in the community. Rebound4Ryan provides activities, mentoring, and lunch for youth in a neighboring community. They also donate to the school for reading programs. Scholarships are provided to high school students in two school districts: Sto Rox and Montour. Please follow us at Rebound4Ryan.com for more information.

THANK YOU

I am deeply indebted and grateful to all the writers who contributed to this book for their tireless efforts and positive engagement in the process. Reliving the worst days of their lives was challenging. Not every mom who I asked was able to participate in the project when I approached them. Some were not yet ready to share their pain and devastation. The grief process sucks. It knocks you out of the world; it brings you down to your knees. I am very proud of those moms who *were* able to share their stories for building resilience and coming out of the dark hole of grief to speak out and radiate love.

I applaud our wonderful kids and marvel at the way they slipped into a new role of helpers from the other side. Their amazing team guided and inspired us throughout our project. Our children are beautiful spirit warriors. They make their mothers proud to be Shining Light parents.

A big heartfelt thank you goes to Elizabeth Boisson, a beautiful mother and the president of Helping Parents Heal, for contributing such an inspiring foreword. Her strength and resilience amaze me. After experiencing the loss of a child twice, she has not only found a way to bounce back to her life but has also built a life-surviving community and helps parents all around the world.

A big special thank you goes to one of the best writers, a beautiful mother, and a professional book editor, Cori Wamsley, who helped me publish my first book *One Year After* and provided professional help and guidance for *The Beauty of a Grieving Mother* as well. I believe that working with a brokenhearted client who speaks broken English was challenging, but Cori nailed it! Also, I would like to express a big heartfelt appreciation to one of Cori's team members Allison Hrip who helped with the edit on this book. She said that, as a mom of three herself, her heart shattered as she journeyed through stories and that each family's experience of signs from the afterlife, courage to keep going, and to keep living and connecting has been a profound encouragement for her. Cori's and Allison's big hearts and compassion have eased the editing part of the project. Thanks to their hard work, the stories of Alina and other beautiful children will live forever through this brilliant book.

Another special thank you goes to our cover designer Karen Captline, who created a beautiful cover that took my breath away the moment I saw it. Karen is also a beautiful, strong-minded woman who radiates love and always has a smile on her face.

I could never find the right words to thank my husband Yan. His true love and deep understanding not only help me move forward in life but also make me thrive. He has supported every move I have taken without judgment. He has accepted the new me and always held me as I have made unexpected changes and pivots trying to navigate my new life. He has always been a role model for our kids, and his strength and perseverance taught them to never give up. Despite what he has been through in life, he never lost the qualities that I admire. I am grateful for having him by my side; without my dear, loving husband, I would not survive a single day of my new life. This book is his book as well.

Also, I would like to express my deepest love and gratitude to all my family and friends for their great compassion and continued support. I am blessed to be a grandmother of our beautiful Angelina, who keeps me on my toes, and I am forever grateful for having my son Artem and his loving and caring wife Ekaterina in my life.

Dear Shining Light Parents! With all my heart, I encourage you to write. Even though you might find putting your emotions into words challenging, I promise that you also will experience joy and find peace. I know how therapeutic writing can be. It helps you move through the grieving process. By writing your stories, you release your negative energies, and that will help you heal.

Please remember that by dedicating your writing to your child, you honor your child's life. So, open up your heart and let their energy in! Feel that deep love and connection with your son or your daughter. Remember that in 50–60 years, you will not be here, but the sound of your child's voice will continue ringing through the pages of your book. Your child's name will never be forgotten. And I KNOW your child being forgotten is the biggest fear of all grieving parents.

So dear moms, share your child's life, express your love by writing your story, and show the world how beautiful you are, both as a woman and as a mother. No matter how hard that is, you are still breathing, so keep walking this unimaginable journey, carrying your beautiful child in your heart. You are a true inspiration of love and strength to all other mothers on earth. And your Shining Light Child is proudly shouting "thank you" from Heaven.

The Beauty of a Grieving Mother

Losing a child is the
biggest fear of any parent.

But *The Beauty of a Grieving
Mother* is NOT about fear.

In this anthology, ten broken-hearted mothers
step ahead of their fears and share their life
stories about love, courage, hope, and survival
after the loss of their child. These mothers
have different lifestyles and backgrounds. Their
children left in different ways and at different
ages. These women grieve differently. But what
they share is the deepest feeling of love for
their beautiful children and a strong desire to
continue their legacies.

When you grieve the loss of a child you develop
a brand new feeling where pain and joy coexist.
They intermingle. They become inseparable.
The beauty of that unique feeling is that
the ugly pain makes the joy profound. Your
suffering makes you feel a deep gratitude.

The pain of a grieving mother is beautiful, but
nobody can grasp it but the grieving mother.

Find strength, love, and beauty in the stories of
these mothers and their children.

Though the journey after
the loss of a child may feel
lonely, **it is not one that
must be traveled alone.**

Elly
Sheykhet

Camille
Dan

Ramona
Vizitiu

E Michelle
Bennett

Claudia
Neagu

Tammy
Osche

Angela
Novak

Shari
Keenan Ramirez

Holly
Wood Tod

Tracy
Montesano

ISBN 9781623751937

90000

9 781623 751937